The Twin Cities of
St. Paul and
Minneapolis

Association of American Geographers

Comparative Metropolitan Analysis Project

Vol. 1   Contemporary Metropolitan America: Twenty Geographical Vignettes.
Cambridge: Ballinger Publishing Company, 1976.

Vol. 2.   Urban Policymaking and Metropolitan Dynamics: A Comparative Geographical Analysis. Cambridge: Ballinger Publishing Company, 1976.

Vol. 3.   A Comparative Atlas of America's Great Cities: Twenty Metropolitan
Regions. Minneapolis: University of Minnesota Press, 1976.

Vignettes of the following metropolitan regions are also published by Ballinger
Publishing Company as separate monographs:

- Boston
- New York-New Jersey
- Philadelphia
- Hartford-Central Connecticut
- Baltimore
- New Orleans
- Chicago
- St. Paul-Minneapolis
- Seattle
- Miami
- Los Angeles

Research Director:
   John S. Adams, University of Minnesota

Associate Director and Atlas Editor:
   Ronald Abler, Pennsylvania State University

Chief Cartographer:
   Ki–Suk Lee, University of Minnesota

Steering Committee and Editorial Board:
   Brian J.L. Berry, Chairman, University of Chicago
   John R. Borchert, University of Minnesota
   Frank E. Horton, Southern Illinois University
   J. Warren Nystrom, Association of American Geographers
   James E. Vance, Jr., University of California, Berkeley
   David Ward, University of Wisconsin

Supported by a grant from the National Science Foundation.

The Twin Cities of St. Paul and Minneapolis

Ronald Abler
The Pennsylvania State University

John S. Adams
John R. Borchert
University of Minnesota

Ballinger Publishing Company ● Cambridge, Massachusetts
A Subsidiary of J.B. Lippincott Company

 This book is printed on recycled paper.

International Standard Book Number: 0-88410-434-6

Library of Congress Catalog Card Number: 76-4801

Printed in the United States of America

Library of Congress Cataloging in Publication Data

Abler, Ronald.
   The Twin Cities of St. Paul and Minneapolis.

   Bibliography: p.
   1. St. Paul—Social conditions. 2. Minneapolis—Social conditions. 3. Cities and towns—Growth. 4. Urbanization—Minnesota—St. Paul. 5. Urbanization—Minnesota—Minneapolis. I. Adams, John S., 1938– joint author. II. Borchert, John R., joint author. III. Title.
HN80.S3A24   309.1'776'57905   76-4801
ISBN 0-88410-434-6

Contents

List of Figures

Images, Identities, and Daily Life

People who have never lived in the Twin Cities depend on visits, friends, and the media for their impressions of the place. Twin Cities residents create their own images, influenced by the same media that inform outsiders. For both groups, the Twin Cities is the Upper Midwest capital, the commercial and transportation gateway to the northwest United States. It is also a sprawling dual-centered metropolis of almost two million persons, enjoying all the advantages that large size permits yet suffering few of the problems that plague older, higher density, single center metropolises with their frequent histories of sharp cultural cleavages. It is a place of surprisingly uniform tastes and a sense that civic problems generally come in manageable proportions.

GEOGRAPHY

The terrain of the Twin Cities region was sculptured by recent glacial activity that left numerous depressions and debris piles that are now lakes and hills. Minneapolis and St. Paul lie on flat areas of sand and gravel washed out from the edges of ice sheets, but they are surrounded by rougher areas left when the glaciers were stationary or retreating rapidly. Local relief in rougher areas averages 200 feet. The glaciers also left swamps, bogs, and sloughs that are ideal breeding places for mosquitos. Despite valiant efforts to control them, mosquitos preclude late evening use of yards and parks for any but the most active or urgent recreations. Unless it is cool or a strong breeze is blowing, mosquitos will drive most people indoors after sundown.

Thanks to the frequent exchange of air, the low population densities, and the small amount of heavy industry in the area, air quality in the Twin Cities is unsurpassed by any United States metropolitan area of over a million people. Temperatures are something else. Over a weather record of 150 years, 108°F in July 1936 was the highest temperature recorded; the lowest reached –41°F in January 1888. In a typical July the temperature stays below 94°F on nine days out of ten and below 85°F on half the days. In a typical January the coldest temperature is above zero on over half the days and stays above –12°F on nine days out of ten. Daily high temperatures normally range from about zero to 38°F in January and from 72 to 94°F in July. The brilliant blue sky on many of the coldest winter days provides an uplift that has no analogue on a steamy July afternoon. Fog is rare. The season of clearer skies but more rain, coming in evening and nighttime showers, runs from early April through September. Winter is drier with only light snow coming from overcast skies. The area has prepared itself for any weather extreme and pays little attention to conditions that would bring many cities to a standstill.

Although the Twin Cities suffer the coldest winters of any major North American metropolis, the bad news is often exaggerated. Many Americans confuse Minneapolis with Minnesota and conclude that the cold winter termperatures in the northern part of the state are typical of the Twin Cities. Actually, when it gets cold in the Twin Cities it usually gets almost as cold in many other cities in the northern United States. Minnesota is a large state, and the distance of places like Bemidji and International Falls, Minnesota, from the Twin Cities is about the same as the distance from Washington, D.C., to Canada, or from New York City to the interior of Maine.

Two kinds of air masses alternate in the Twin Cities. One is cool, clear Canadian air which makes many summer days so perfect and the winter so cold. The other comes from the Pacific Ocean, passing over the Rockies and warming as it descends moving eastward. This air produces warm sunny winter days ideal for outdoor sports. On rare occasions, maritime tropical air from the Gulf of Mexico reaches the Twin Cities at the surface bringing hot humid weather. However, even in the summer Gulf air reaches the area less than 10 percent of the time, even though it predominates in the summer over states as near as Illinois and Missouri. In the Twin Cities, tropical Gulf air frequently overrides the cooler air at the surface and brings evening and nighttime showers.

Even rarer is the occasional summer arrival of air from the Hudson Bay region, holding daytime temperatures in the 60s with accompanying rains, and prompting much discussion and wonder. Summer skies are fair 73 percent of the time, and up to 85 percent of the time during the last three weeks of July. The most common time for thundershowers is around midnight. Summer air in the Twin Cities is usually not tropical air and lacks the moisture content typical over much of the United States. Despite the high latitude (45°), the early summer sun in the Twin Cities is closer to being overhead than it is at the equator. Also, because of the latitude and daylight savings time, the early summer sun sets well after 9:00 P.M., making it possible to read a newspaper out of doors until 9:30 P.M.

Autumn, or Indian Summer, offers fair skies 68 percent of the time, with mild dry days, cool evenings, and only occasional light rain likely at night. This extended period of sunny days has a special beauty for early risers. Twin City lakes are still warm from the summer sun, so when night air cools below its dewpoint gossamer streamers of early morning fog form over the lakes. They rise only a few feet above the water but give added beauty to fiery sunrises over red and orange trees beneath the purple dawn sky. Many residents insist this is the finest season of all.

Early November through December brings the holiday season. The snows begin but fail to last, for the ground is still warm. Around December 10 the snow becomes permanent and most lakes and streams freeze over. This is also the cloudiest season of the year, but the clouds insure the maintenance of the snow cover, enhancing the holiday atmosphere. Visitors during this snow white season are surprised that they can see almost as well outside at night as during the day.

Real winter lasts from New Year's Day to mid-February. Skies clear and the sun shines on the permanent snow cover. Average high temperatures hover around 13°F and winter sports reach full tempo. Ice skaters dot the frozen lakes, skiers dot the low hills, and outside the central cities snowmobilers race across frozen lakes and along roadside trails. The transition to spring starts in mid-February and lasts through March. It is the snowiest part of the year but the snows never last long.

Spring comes suddenly, melting the snow and raising temperatures abruptly to the 70s by May. In early April, following cold front passages, passing showers fall from small thunderclouds forming behind the fronts. These attractive but fast-moving April clouds may bring as many as five brief showers in a single day with sunshine between. Spring—or what passes for it—surprises newcomers to the Twin Cities. Most other major cities lie near major bodies of water which slow down the spring warm-up. In those places lake and sea breezes turn many days that begin warm into cool ones. Twin Cities lakes while often deep are too small and scattered to affect the temperature. They warm quickly in the spring as the Twin Cities warm up.

THE PEOPLE

Complementing a north woods, theater of seasons image is the notion that the Twin Cities are populated by blonde Swedes. Scandinavian-language vaudeville teams that worked out of the Twin Cities at the turn of the century started the image of Minneapolis as New Stockholm. Similarly, Sinclair Lewis's *Main Street,* with its portrayal of Yankee-Scandinavian conflicts, reinforced the idea that Minnesota and the Twin Cities are predominantly Scandinavian.

One does occasionally encounter a Swede or Norwegian in the Twin Cities, but ethnicity is a leitmotiv rather than a dominant chord. Time is one explanation of feeble ethnicity. There are indeed twenty-six pages of Johnsons in the Minneapolis telephone book, but most are second and third generation Americans and many are black. Young persons today may acknowledge their ethnic origins, invoking echnicity for personal identificational reasons. The importance of Scandinavian foreign stock in the Twin Cities was probably exaggerated to begin with and the exaggeration has increased as the foreign-born groups aged and died. In 1970, the total foreign *stock* (foreign-born plus persons with one or both parents foreign-born) amounted to 17.7 percent of the metropolitan population, but foreign-*born* were only 3.0 percent of the population. Moreover, the foreign stock has never been dominated by any single group. Swedish foreign stock was largest at 3.1 percent of the 1970 population, followed by Germans (2.7 percent), and Norwegians (2.2 percent). No other group except Canadians accounts for 1.0 percent of the Twin Cities population. All Scandinavians lumped together (Swedish, Norwegian, Danish, and Finnish) are but 6.1 percent of the metropolitan population.

This does not imply a complete absence of visible ethnic concentrations, but with few exceptions—such as northeast Minneapolis (Slavic) or the "West Side" of St. Paul (Chicano)—they are well hidden. In 1970 there were about 16,500 people "of Spanish language" in the Twin Cities, of whom no more than 500 were Puerto Rican in origin.

Dispersal also dilutes ethnicity. Census tracts in which more than a fifth of the population consists of foreign stock are rare. Weak ethnic concentrations persist in the Twin Cities but the prosperity of the first and second generations promotes dispersal throughout the metropolitan region. Annual celebrations such as Svenskarnas Dag (Swedish Day), Syttendae Mai (May 17, Norweigan Constitution Day), and St. Patrick's Day (St. Paul only) are well attended, but beyond such well-publicized, highly commercialized events, ethnicity is a sometime thing.

The ethnic homogeneity of the Twin Cities is matched by racial homogeneity. Nonwhites numbered 50,000 in 1970, of whom 32,000 were black. Blacks constituted 1.8 percent of the Twin Cities population; the remaining nonwhites were native Americans (Indians) and Orientals. Almost 10,000 Indians enumerated by the 1970 census form one of the larger metropolitan Indian populations in the nation.

The population of these middle class cities seem well endowed with the attitudes and attributes that bring material success in the American system. The 1969 median family income of $11,680 was well above the $9,590 median for SMSAs over 200,000 population. Only 4.6 percent of Twin Cities families fall below the 1969 poverty level as opposed to 8.5 percent in all metropolitan areas. At the same time, the average income is not raised by the small number of very high incomes; 6.2 percent of the nation's families had 1969 incomes exceeding $25,000, compared with 5.6 percent of all Twin Cities families. Without minimizing the extent of poverty in the Twin Cities, the fact remains that residents are well off economically. The sharp cultural and social gradients that foster tension and conflict in many cities are absent in Minneapolis and St. Paul, producing a metropolis in which social and cultural conflict has rarely attained the proportions it has in other places.

Crime rates are relatively low, the proportion of draftees and enlistees rejected as mentally or physically unsuited for military service has always been low, and education levels and incomes are above national averages. The region's social ethos and general conviction that problems are solvable is evident in the politicians it elects at all levels of government. The progressive image of New Deal Governor Floyd B. Olson, for example, and the violent but successful Teamsters strike of 1934, reflect an abiding grassroots social concern and activism that has often been translated into legislative innovation backed by a willingness to provide concrete backing for education and social legislation. Hubert Humphrey, for example, enjoyed widespread political popularity in the Twin Cities in a political career that began as mayor of Minneapolis. Right down to the local level there is a spirit of openness and honesty in political affairs. The electorate expects open, honest, and efficient government and their expectations are usually fulfilled.

THE "TWIN" CITIES

Failing to distinguish between the two cities is the greatest gap between external image and internal reality. For most nonresidents and for 99 percent of all Minneapolis residents, Minneapolis *is* the Twin Cities (Figure 1). Air travelers are sold tickets to Minneapolis, they board planes going to Minneapolis, and are informed en route of their estimated arrival time in Minneapolis. Should the flight continue beyond

Minneapolis, responding to the question, "Are you going to Minneapolis?" with, "No, I'm going to St. Paul" will elicit an ill-concealed sneer from the cabin attendant putting "occupied" signs on through passengers' seats. Dignitaries visiting St. Paul often insult their hosts with an opening comment on "How nice it is to be in Minneapolis (again)." A St. Paul newspaper columnist keeps score on how often St. Paul facilities are mislocated in Minneapolis and vice versa. At last report, the score stood heavily in favor of Minneapolis. The frequency with which St. Paul is incorporated into Minneapolis and the rarity with which

Figure 1. Minneapolis at the Falls of St. Anthony. Grain elevators and ancient milling facilities of General Mills on the far (west) side of the falls and the Pillsbury A Mill on the east side (lower right) commemorate the city's turn of the century livelihood. A sea of parking lots (right center) marks the Gateway renewal area leveled in the 1950s and vigorously rebuilding.

people in Minneapolis think they are in St. Paul dramatizes how people fail to note that St. Paul is a separate city (Figure 2).

Minneapolis and St. Paul are distinct places. They are not identical twins nor are they fraternal, having been founded twenty years and ten miles apart. They started as neighboring rivals but ended up Siamese twins. St. Paul and Minneapolis are inescapably tied by proximity and, like the unhappy Chang and Eng, they sometimes fight. Interurban rivalry no longer generates the silliness and bitterness it produced in the nineteenth century, but it persists. Short-

ly after major league baseball came to the Twin Cities a joke circulated: "Did you hear that they were going to name the team the Minnehaha Twins instead of the Minnesota Twins? ... Minne- for Minneapolis and -haha for St. Paul." Some Minneapolitans assert that they set their watches back fifty years when they go to St. Paul. St. Paul acquired an inferiority complex when Minneapolis became larger. The feeling persists. St. Paulites disguise their jealousy of their neighbor's taller buildings, larger size, and spruce image with smugness and the unmistakable impression that they are

Figure 2. Downtown St. Paul, bounded by railroad facilities and warehouses near the former mouth of Trout Creek (right edge), Interstates 94 and 35-E (top) and the Capitol Approach area (top left), residential areas (far left), and the Mississippi River (foreground). Industrial land uses occupy the flood plain across the river from downtown on St. Paul's "West Side". Although the Mississippi flows from west to east at downtown St. Paul, its path through the Twin Cities area is generally north-south.

cultured and urbane while Minneapolitans are bumptious philistines, but St. Paul is usually the butt of interurban jokes.

Twin Cities residents often describe the difference between St. Paul and Minneapolis in terms of St. Paul being an older, "Eastern" city like Boston, whereas Minneapolis in its business bustle and commercial vitality is more akin to Chicago or Denver. That characterization is accurate, for it acknowledges ethnic, religious, and geographical differences, along with economic ambitions and visual impressions.

St. Paul's earlier start is evident in the larger size of the German and Irish ethnic groups there. It has larger Irish and German foreign stocks than Minneapolis despite its smaller population. Minneapolis remains more Scandinavian than St. Paul; the Norwegian and Swedish groups constitute almost a tenth of the Minneapolis population. Proportions in other ethnic groups are similar in the two cities. Today's stereotypes are residuals of earlier social structures. In 1930, for example, German foreign stock was 13.9 percent of St. Paul's population but only 7.7 percent of the Minneapolis total. Every fifth Minneapolitan was born in Norway or Sweden or had at least one parent who was; every seventh St. Paulite fell into the same category. The Irish were not an especially large group in either city in 1930, but they were twice as important in St. Paul as in Minneapolis.

Past and present ethnic differences have produced relatively little impact on the urban landscape. Even a genuine Scandinavian restaurant is impossible to find. Denmark, Finland, Norway, and Sweden maintain consulates in Minneapolis but they are offices in large buildings and are outwardly indistinguishable from the law offices that surround them. The Scandinavian nations have no representation in St. Paul. In fact, none of them is listed in the St. Paul phone book. When queried about this the Swedish consulate was uncommunicative; the Norwegian consul observed that his offices were not listed in the Madison, Duluth, or Fargo directories, and therefore he could see no good reason why they should be listed in the St. Paul directory. The German consulate is located in Minneapolis but is listed only in the St. Paul telephone directory. There were almost identical numbers of German foreign stock in Minneapolis and St. Paul in 1970, so whereas

location might be a matter of indifference, it is curious that the consulate is not listed in the city in which it is located. But the score is partially evened out by the Mexican consulate, which is located in St. Paul but listed only in the Minneapolis directory. The American Swedish Institute and the Sons of Norway have headquarters in Minneapolis, but the *Volksfest Kultus Haus* is in St. Paul. The St. Paul Irish have no formal organization, but they make a magnificent impression on the urban landscape during the St. Patrick's Day parade.

Relics of these earlier ethnic concentrations are rapidly disappearing, but the religious and moral differences that derive from the earlier and stronger ethnic differences persist. St. Paulites, being more dominantly Southern German, Austrian, and Irish, tend to be Catholics (37 percent). Local wags often remark that it is fitting that the St. Paul Cathedral stands higher and is more imposing than the state capitol building, for that is, or at least was, an accurate reflection of relationships between the powers the edifices memorialize. In St. Paul, flats and houses are still advertised with no location given other than the name of the Catholic parish in which the dwelling is located. Minneapolis is about as Protestant as St. Paul is Catholic. Lutheranism is the dominant faith; Catholics are 20 percent of the population. The headquarters of the Lutheran Brotherhood Insurance Company and the American Lutheran Church bear substantive witness to the strength of the sect in Minneapolis.

Minneapolitans claim that St. Paul is impossible to navigate. Both Minneapolis and St. Paul are laid out in typically midwestern grid patterns except for their central business districts, where streets are parallel and perpendicular to the river. The river churlishly refuses to flow either north-south or east-west; hence both city centers are surrounded by a ring of confusion where the early, river-oriented streets mesh with the cardinal grid. Matters are complicated by the differing topographies of the central areas. Downtown St. Paul is hilly, with a bluff between downtown and the river and another at the western margin of the central area; downtown Minneapolis is flat. The Minneapolis street system is easy to comprehend. A matrix of numbered streets and avenues with cardinal directions appended creates a cartesian space in which finding addresses is simple. St. Paul's street- and house-numbering scheme can scarcely be described as a system. All streets are named with the exception of a few in the CBD. More importantly, there are far fewer than a hundred numbers per block. Many a visitor has set off to walk the "ten blocks" from downtown to an address at 1000 West, only to learn that more than two miles separate the two. St. Paul house numbers were assigned on the basis of water meter installations along early thoroughfares; thus there are usually about three city blocks per hundred numbers. The combination of named streets and irregular numbering creates different conceptions of space and different orientations. Minneapolis residents identify their locations as points and move from one place to another by mentally constructing their own path between origin and destination. People in St. Paul conceive of their locations as areas or neighborhoods because points are too imprecise. They tend to be route-oriented and in asking or giving directions to a destination they will seek or specify the path to be taken rather than the geometric location. St. Paul is a city that must be memorized; its geography cannot be deduced from the street grid.

Ethnic, religious, and geographical differences ultimately result in differences in information flow that perpetuate those differences. Telephone message flows highlight the existence of two separate cities. None of the largest outgoing flows from Twin Cities telephone exchanges crosses the Minneapolis-St. Paul city boundary, nor do any of the second largest outflows. Only at the level of the third largest outflow is the boundary between the two cities breached, and then only for two exchanges. Newspaper circulation patterns also perpetuate separate identities. The *St. Paul Dispatch* and *Pioneer Press* are delivered in St. Paul but not in Minneapolis. The *Minneapolis Star* and *Tribune*, however, penetrate St. Paul, with daily home delivery available in the western half of the city and in many of the suburbs. The Sunday Minneapolis paper is readily available throughout Ramsey County.

Television and radio also affect regional identity. Announcers on the two major stations are careful to say "St. Paul and Minneapolis" as often as they say "Minneapolis and St. Paul." But other things being equal, Minneapolis and its suburbs still get more air time because of

their larger populations. The major station's (WCCO) studios are in downtown Minneapolis and thus the idle chit-chat of disc jockeys and television announcers almost always concerns events there. Because of WCCO's phenomenally large market penetration, this redounds in the favor of Minneapolis.

Differences between the two cities are real and a visitor ignores them at some peril.

WORKING

The 1970 Twin Cities labor force consisted of 760,000 workers. Thus about 42 percent of the total population and about 62 percent of the population over sixteen years of age drew an income from working, males outnumbering females almost two to one. St. Paul has more jobs in manufacturing and transportation than Minneapolis as a result of its earlier start and more important role as a rail transportation center. Correspondingly, St. Paul has fewer jobs in trade, finance, and services. The location of the state capitol and a number of federal offices in St. Paul puts it ahead of Minneapolis in public administration employment. Differences in occupational structure follow from St. Paul's higher manufacturing employment, but the differences are negligible.

The fifteen largest employers engage a fifth of the metropolitan labor force. Some of them loom disproportionately large in making the Twin Cities different from other places. Local government, including public schools (54,000 employees), the University of Minnesota (20,300, one-third of them part time students), federal government (18,500), and the state of Minnesota (15,000) are four of the top five employers in the area. Other important employers include 3M (16,900), Honeywell (13,000), Control Data (10,700), Dayton-Hudson Corporation (10,000), Univac Division of Sperry Rand Corporation (8,800), Northwestern Bell Telephone Company (8,200), Burlington-Northern (6,500), Northwest Airlines (4,700), Northern States Power Company (4,000), General Mills (3,100), and Federal Cartridge (3,000).

Making a living is likely to involve a medium length trip to work because of the Twin Cities low population density and dispersed employment centers. Only 12 percent of the jobs are located in the central business districts; most are located in the remainder of the central cities and in the first tier of suburbs in Hennepin and Ramsey Counties. At the same time, the existence of two CBDs acts to reduce distance to work despite low density by splitting central employment and thereby putting it closer to more people.

PLAYING

Although the work ethic is alive and well in the Twin Cities, all work and no play make a dull boy. But there is little danger of Twin Cities residents becoming dullards. They play hard, whether they do so by watching other people or whether they are active in sports, pastimes, and festivals. The region and the local ethos offer many opportunities for individual and communal recreation.

Nonresidents are likely to be most familiar with the organized hoopla of the St. Paul Winter Carnival and the summer Minneapolis Aquatennial; local boosters insure that each receives some national publicity. The Winter Carnivals started before World War I and have waxed and waned in elaborateness since. Minneapolis chafed for years at the success of the Winter Carnival and in the 1940s, unable to tolerate the affront to its dignity any longer, established the Aquatennial. The Aquatennial Parade occurs downtown, but the rest of the festival is dispersed throughout the city's network of lakes and parks.

Smaller festivals and celebrations include St. Patrick's Day in St. Paul, with a parade and green beer. Rice Street and Payne Avenue in St. Paul have sponsored annual festivals for years, the former with a Swedish accent and the latter with an Italian flavor. Minnehaha Park in Minneapolis is the traditional location for annual Norwegian and Swedish celebrations. Recently the "Snoose Boulevard" festival has recreated the aura of the turn of the century designation of Cedar Avenue as Snoose Boulevard, an uncomplimentary recognition of a Scandinavian preference for chewing snuff. The summer ends with the Minnesota State Fair, a twelve day event drawing well over a million persons from throughout the state.

The Twin Cities offer a normal quota of spectator sports. Major league baseball, football, hockey, and tennis provide year round diversion for professional sports buffs. Major league culture is also much in evidence and remarkably well patronized. The Minnesota Or-chestra gives three subscription concerts a week (two in Minneapolis, one in St. Paul) during its regular season, and the Tyrone Guthrie Theatre presents eight performances a week during its season. In addition to the Minnesota Orchestra and the Guthrie, the St. Paul Chamber Orchestra, and many other orchestras, chamber groups, choruses, opera companies, and theatre companies perform throughout the year.

When Sir Tyrone Guthrie selected Minneapolis as the site for his repertoire theatre, he established the Twin Cities as a theatrical center of unusual proportion. About thirty theatres operate in the Twin Cities, making the area a major attraction for young actors and actresses. This abundance of acting talent has attracted increasing numbers of national advertising agencies to establish branches in Minneapolis to use this wealth of talent.

The Twin Cities' physical setting provides opportunities for participant play in greater abundance than is the case in most metropolitan regions. Fishing is legal for some species year round and the region around the Twin Cities is studded with lakes and rivers that provide adequate to excellent fishing. About a fourth of the adult populations of Hennepin and Ramsey counties fish. A common catch from local lakes includes panfish and northern pike. The latter can get as large as twenty pounds or more. Although specimens that size are increasingly rare within the metropolitan area, game fishermen hook sizable northerns often enough to make fishing for them exciting and worthwhile. Bass fishing at many lakes in the metropolitan area (including lakes within the central cities) is excellent; five pound bass are caught daily and larger ones are not especially newsworthy. The Mississippi and Minnesota rivers yield giant catfish, bass, northern pike, and walleyed pike (Minnesota's premier fish).

Boating, whether incidental to fishing or an end in itself, is also popular. In early 1974, 142,000 boats of all kinds were licensed to residents of Hennepin and Ramsey counties. There are remarkably few accidents and fistfights given the number of craft on the water, but increased boating pressure on the metropolitan area's lakes will eventually lead to zoned use.

Moving through space effortlessly is a delight that knows no seasonal bounds, and snowmobiles make it possible to do so in the winter, relieving the winter doldrums for the motorboat enthusiast. There were 85,000 snowmobiles licensed to metropolitan residents in 1974, one snowmobile for every twenty-three people. For comparison, there is one boat for every twelve people. Snowmobiles create conflicts. Farmers and property owners adjacent to open areas object to having their property overrun and their tranquility disrupted by the noisy devices, as do cross-country skiers, ice fishermen, and other seekers of outdoor winter quiet. The antagonisms between ice fishermen and snowmobile fans arise because the frozen lakes are the best places to race snowmobiles, most of which will easily go fifty miles per hour, with top speeds for powerful models of seventy or eighty miles per hour.

Twin Cities residents make heavy use of their metropolitan area for outdoor recreation, sometimes creating a nuisance for one another. Voluntary and legislated zoning, rationing, or pricing of lakes, campgrounds, and other facilities when overtaxed will make the region more pleasant for all potential users. For the foreseeable future, high quality fishing, small game hunting, hiking, camping, cross-country and downhill skiing, sailing, and water skiing will continue to be available no more than forty-five minutes drive from the doorstep of any Twin Cities resident.

The Twin Cities area, with about 10 percent of the public ballrooms in the United States, offers an unusual opportunity for young and old. Typically, Friday night's band plays rock and popular music, while on Saturday night and Sunday afternoon it turns to polka and waltz music. The rock crowd tends to be young, but the old-time group is a mixture of ages since many natives and migrants to the area learn to polka and waltz before they are ten years old.

THE GOOD LIFE IN A GOOD PLACE

Unless childhood was a totally dismal experience, a person's hometown remains the best place in the world. Natives hold fond memories of places others abhor. Nevertheless, our collective experience with the Twin Cities and other metropolitan areas encourages the conclusion that the Twin Cities are a better than average place to live. The continental climate serves up winter hardships, summer irritations, and a niggardly spring, but it also produces marked seasonal changes that most residents find bracing. Climate and topography combine to offer nearby recreational opportunities in an abundance and variety few cities can match. A wide range of low density, single family housing alternatives on well-maintained elm-lined streets enables most households to find the housing they want at the location they prefer at reasonable cost. People themselves are well educated and confident. Visitors usually notice an atmosphere of openness and friendliness, a pleasant contrast to the anxieties or desperation of their own cities. Twin Cities residents are bemused by assertions that their amiability is a result of being a decade or so behind Chicago, Los Angeles, and New York. They are cosmopolitan enough to disbelieve that such is the case and self-assured enough to prefer remaining the way they are.

Minnesota was featured as "The State that Works" in a cover story in the August 13, 1973, issue of *Time*. State politics had much to do with the article, yet the essay was a sensible and sensitive portrayal of the state and the metropolitan area. Things *do* work in Minnesota and the Twin Cities and that asset seems to distinguish the metropolitan area from many others. People having business with public officials or private concerns expect their transactions to be accomplished promptly and efficiently, and they usually are. Pettifogging is minimal, whether the business at hand is licensing a canoe or buying a house. Twin Cities residents grouse about the day-to-day irritations of life, but bitterness and despair are rare. The freedom from the hundreds of weekly anxieties and squabbles characteristic of cities in which the average person expects to be gulled every time he or she turns around is perhaps the most refreshing element of Twin Cities life. People feel that life and events are manageable and under control, and they are usually right.

The First Century

The Twin Cities were born in the 1840s, and at least one of the twins was conceived in sin. Civilian settlement was illegal in the St. Paul area before 1837 and before 1851 in Minneapolis because Indian cessions had not yet been obtained. Military authorities at Fort Snelling winked at occasional squatters on the military reservation at the junction of the Minnesota and Mississippi rivers, however, and by the late 1830s several commercial enterprises were established near the fort (Figure 3). A soldier's payday recreation was the same then as now; fifty of the fort's troops spent the night of June 30, 1839, in the guardhouse after visiting Brown's Groggery. Thereupon the fort's martinet commander, Major Plympton, determined to rid the fort of the fleshly attractions purveyed by civilian merchants. After blustering for a year he evicted 150 civilians from the west bank of the river in May 1840. The evictees moved downriver on the east bank to Pig's Eye, the nickname of an earlier refugee publican who had set up shop in a cave. The embryonic village was supplied with a more euphonious name a year later when a log chapel dedicated to St. Paul was erected by Father Lucien Galtier, but St. Paul residents are fond of their disreputable origins.

St. Paul's lusty conception might suggest that the Twin Cities are a happenstance of history, but that is not so. Given the nation's developing economy and the way settlement was spreading, the rise of a great city on the site of St. Paul-Minneapolis was inevitable.

By 1840 American settlement had crossed the Mississippi into what is now Iowa, Missouri, and Kansas, and steam navigation had converted the Ohio-Mississippi-Missouri river network into an efficient transportation system over which goods and people could be shipped quickly and cheaply. The Indian cessions of 1837 opened the St. Croix country at the same time that demand for the region's logs and lumber was growing in the areas to the south that could be reached by river transportation. Entrepreneurs were quick to exploit the "pineries" penetrated by the St. Croix and Rum rivers (Figure 4). Sawmills were established at Marine on the St. Croix (1839), Stillwater (1844), and St. Anthony (1848) and forest products soon became a mainstay of the region's export economy. The territory's extensive timber resources and great agricultural potential guaranteed that Minnesota would prosper, but a more specific set of circumstances guaranteed the emergence of the St. Paul-Minneapolis complex.

St. Paul, with a gradually sloping access through the bluffs to the uplands north of the river bend, became the practical head of navigation on the upper Mississippi, and the Falls of St. Anthony, ten miles upstream, was the largest water power site west of Niagara. River transportation was crucial over the next several decades. St. Paul offered a convenient transfer point before the Mississippi River entered a gorge upstream from Fort Snelling and became impassible at the falls (Figure 5). As a consequence it became the region's first major com-

Figure 3. Fort Snelling, 1844. A significant landmark in the history of Minnesota and the Northwest, the fort was established in 1819 at the Junction of the Minnesota and Mississippi rivers. It effectively extended the authority of the young American nation over the region and paved the way for white settlement. This water color by J.C. Wild shows the Henry H. Sibley house in the foreground and the buildings of the Indian agency behind the post. The painting is in the Minnesota Historical Society collection. Photo courtesy of the Minnesota Historical Society.

mercial center. Meanwhile, sawmilling and flour milling, soon to become the region's dominant industries, got their start largely at St. Anthony Falls where a sixty-five foot drop in the river provided a ready source of power (Figure 6). The ten miles separating the two guaranteed the development of twin cities. A slow riverboat trip might take half a day. Even a trip on the early railroads took forty-five minutes to an hour. The distance separating the cities made consolidation unthinkable given the overland transportation technology of the 1840s and 1850s. Their successful separate development precluded consolidation long before a city ten miles in breadth became thinkable.

In the earliest days the region offered the American and international economies furs and timber. Both were important to the infant Twin

Cities. Furs had been a standby of regional production since 1650. Yields were declining by the 1830s, but enough production and trade persisted to provide an early boost for St. Paul, making the city one of the world's major fur centers into the twentieth century. As fashions changed and demand for beaver declined, buffalo hides became more important and the fur frontier shifted into northwestern Minnesota and the Dakota Territory. Traders from the Red River region brought their furs to St. Paul by oxcart in the summer and dogsled in the winter. There they were exchanged for provisions and manufactured goods brought upriver by steamboat. Trade with the Red River country and with surrounding settlements supported St. Paul until the designation of the city as the territorial capital in 1849. St. Paul be-

Figure 4. Minnesota vegetation at the time of European settlement. Hardwood forests surrounded the sites of the Twin Cities and separated the fertile prairie lands southwest from the virgin pine forests in the northeast. The river systems into the pineries delivered logs to sawmills at St. Anthony, Stillwater, and Marine, kicking off a major export industry.

came the state capital in 1858, assuring continuing success.

St. Anthony (the part of Minneapolis east of the Mississippi) started late compared to other sawmilling centers. A mill had been built at St. Anthony Falls in the 1820s to provide Fort Snelling with lumber and squatters settled in the area intermittently. Major Plympton usually evicted them, not, it would appear, because he was sensitive to legal proprieties, but rather because he and a partner had designs on the site. His efforts came to naught, for a sharp operator from the St. Croix, Franklin Steele, managed

to prove a claim on the site and sawmilling and settlement commenced in 1849. Loggers sent timber from the north down the Rum and Mississippi rivers to the mills at St. Anthony.

Nobody familiar with the region had any doubts concerning St. Anthony's ultimate fortunes. The magnificent power site made it clear that a great manufacturing city would develop there. Moreover, Nicollet Island, just above the falls, split the river into two relatively narrow channels and thus provided a bridge site superior to any other in the vicinity. But St. Anthony's growth was retarded for a few more

Figure 5. St. Paul, 1855. When S. Holmes Andrews painted this oil of St. Paul in 1855, the population of the city was less than 5,000. It was a year of unprecedented immigration. Boats brought approximately 30,000 passengers to the Minnesota capital and from there they funneled out to other parts of the territory. Andrews' view of St. Paul shows the Mississippi River in the foreground and the territorial Capitol and First Presbyterian Church in the center and right background. Nothing is known about this artist whose painting is one of the prized items in the Minnesota Historical Society's collections. Photo courtesy of the Minnesota Historical Society.

years because Steele had trouble raising the capital he needed to develop the falls. The area across the river was not opened for settlement until 1851 and conditions remained confused for four years thereafter as squatters and land speculators pressed their conflicitng claims. In 1855 the situation was clarified. All of Hennepin County (which had been organized in 1852), was declared preemption territory: the squatters'claims were recognized. A building boom ensued and on the west side of the river the city of Minneapolis was incorporated in 1856. Steele's Minneapolis Bridge Company opened its suspension bridge over the Mississippi on July 4, 1855, signaling the beginning of the end for St. Anthony. Even though it was detached from Ramsey County and added to Hennepin County in 1856, maintaining a separate corporate existence until 1872, Minneapolis quickly overtook St. Anthony after 1860.

The rivalry of the early centers for political power and population growth is still evident in the locations of state institutions. St. Paul had been designated as capital when the Minnesota Territory was established in 1849, and the state capital remained there despite attempts by land speculators to shift it to St. Peter when statehood was granted in 1858. Stillwater and St. Anthony, naturally envious of St. Paul's good fortune, were mollified when the state penitentiary and the state university were established in 1851. Stillwater, being larger and more influential, got the prison, which appeared to be more lucrative than the university at that time. St. Anthony was designated the site of the university, which did little for St. Anthony in the period before it was incorporated into Minneapolis, but which has been of inestimable importance to Minneapolis and the Twin Cities over the years. St. Peter's

Figure 6. St. Anthony Falls. This painting of the east channel of the Mississippi River in 1857 shows the booming little town of St. Anthony, built close to the falls, as well as the picturesque wildness of the river scenery below the town. On the left is Hennepin Island, with its flour mills and the sluice which carried lumber from sawmills below the rapids for rafting to the lower river. The Winslow House, a well-known early hotel, dominates the hill in the background and in the right foreground stands a wood products factory. The artist painted the town at the high spot in its development, for St. Anthony never recovered from the financial panic which hit only a few months after the picture was painted. In 1872 St. Anthony was combined with Minneapolis, its prosperous rival across the river. Ferdinand Reichardt (1819–1895) was a Danish-born landscape artist who was especially noted for his paintings of Niagara Falls. The original oil is owned by the Minnesota Historical Society. Photo courtesy of the Minnesota Historical Society.

interests were finally acknowledged when an insane asylum was built there in 1866.

Earlier rivalries are also still evident within the Twin Cities themselves. Despite the development of an uninterrupted urban fabric, St. Paul, St. Anthony, and Minneapolis each developed its own residential district for the wealthy. The distances between centers and nineteenth century transportation make St. Paul's separate development understandable, but the early separation of St. Anthony's patrician families from the Minneapolis latecomers is explained by the river obstacle and a single congested bridge across it. After additional perma-

nent bridges were opened in 1873, at Plymouth Avenue upstream from the falls and at 10th Avenue South below the falls, the St. Anthony upper classes began migrating west of the river.

RAPID SETTLEMENT AND URBAN GROWTH, 1860 to 1890

Sawmills, flour mills, banking, railroads, settlement, immigration, agricultural production, and the development of the Twin Cities are so closely intertwined that it is impossible to say which caused which. Growth or change in any one had immediate repercussions for the others.

The repercussions in turn fed more change. Railroads, for example, were chronically short of capital. Yet they had extensive land grants that could be converted to capital if settlers were available to take up the land. Immigrants wanted land, but often had no way of reaching available lands until cheap railroad transportation became available. Once settled and engaged in commercial agriculture, immigrants relied on rail transportation and Twin Cities traders to supply them with manufactured products and imported foodstuffs and on Twin Cities processors to buy their export production. As the Twin Cities prospered from trade, transportation, sawmilling, and flour milling, they took pains to extend the railroads, promote immigration and settlement, and serve as the major market and processing center for the region's agricultural exports. Once such a cycle began, Eastern, European, and Canadian capitalists were eager to provide the investment needed to keep the cycle going. Through a series of such cycles, the entire state was settled between 1860 and 1890 and the population of the Twin Cities increased from 13,000 to 300,000 during the same period.

Railroads were planned during the 1850s but persistent difficulties in obtaining capital prevented actual construction until 1862, when a track was completed between St. Paul and St. Anthony. Five years later the tracks were extended to St. Cloud under the auspices of the St. Paul and Pacific Railroad. Railroad construction continued intermittently throughout the 1870s, and in 1871 a number of important links were completed. The Northern Pacific finished its line between St. Paul and Duluth, providing the Twin Cities with water access to the East. A direct link to Chicago that ran by way of Tomah, Wisconsin, was also finished. Indirect connection with Chicago had existed since 1867. Perhaps most important of all, lines to Breckenridge and Moorhead in the Red River valley were completed in 1871, thus opening the valley to settlement and giving the Twin Cities access to its produce. By 1887 tracks were completed through North Dakota to Great Falls, Montana, and the Twin Cities were first linked with Seattle in 1883.

Railroads from the East Coast had reached Chicago in 1852 and Rock Island in 1854. Thereafter they were increasingly important channels for domestic and overseas immigrants to Minnesota who could travel by train to Rock Island and then by steamer to St. Paul. Foreign

immigration accelerated during the 1860s, but the real boom was to come after the Civil War, when direct rail connection to eastern and Great Lakes ports was established. In 1860 native-born persons comprised two-thirds of Minnesota's residents, most of whom had come from the Midwest, New York, Pennsylvania, and New England. By 1880 native-born residents constituted less than one-third of the state's population. Most of the newcomers had come from Scandinavia, Germany, Canada, and Ireland. Recognition of the need for settlers was widespread. The state government established an immigration bureau in 1867. The railroads started their own about the same time. Agents in Europe and in East Coast seaports publicized the state with lyrical descriptions of its fertility and prosperity. More importantly, they arranged ship passage from Europe, met immigrants in ports, housed them while their through passage into the interior was being arranged, and then dispatched them directly to Minnesota's waiting lands.

Until 1870, agricultural settlement was mainly confined to the hardwood forest zone extending from southeastern to north central Minnesota. Settlement of the prairies awaited railroad expansion into the grasslands and solid evidence that prairie land could be successfully cultivated, for it was widely believed that grasslands were less fertile than forest lands.

Demand for wheat helped fuel the drive to settle Minnesota and the Dakotas. Whereas earlier settlers might have spent several years engaged in subsistence agriculture before building up their production to the point that production for sale absorbed most of their efforts, the wheat bonanza of the 1870s brought in bonanza wheat farmers—Yankees using eastern risk capital to develop railroad lands for agriculture. Immigrants followed in the 1880s, steadily expanding the cultivated acreage. Increases in the proportion of cultivated acreage in wheat assumed boom proportions after 1870 for several reasons. Railroads were bringing fresh lands into reach as they marched westward, and wheat offered the kind of immediate return on limited investment that was especially welcome given the frontier's limited capital. Another incentive was the availability of mechanical reapers and threshers that made it possible to harvest acreages that would have been unthinkable two decades earlier. Improved plows and demonstrated success quickly overcame lingering resistance to farming prairies and most of the Minnesota grasslands south of Moorhead were taken up between 1870 and 1880. Finally, and perhaps most important of all, new milling techniques made it possible and desirable to use the hard spring wheats that grew especially well in Minnesota.

Prior to the 1870s wheat was ground between stone wheels, and soft winter wheat was the premium breadstuff because it produced a much better flour than spring wheat. But winter wheat often died during Minnesota's bitter winters. Spring wheat has a hard bran (shell) that shatters during milling. Before 1870 it was virtually impossible to separate the bran from the flour, so there was little demand for hard wheat flour. Purifiers developed in Minnesota and applied on a large scale in Minneapolis transformed the industry by turning spring wheat into the premium breadstuff. It was more nutritious than winter wheat, and after some other milling problems were overcome by replacing millstones with steel and porcelain rollers, spring wheat commanded a higher price than winter wheat.

St. Paul rail men and Minneapolis millers were at the forefront of railroad extension, settlement expansion, and milling innovation. St. Paul's James J. Hill organized the Great Northern Railway out of the old St. Paul and Pacific in 1878. The Northern Pacific line to Duluth provided access to the Great Lakes and thus to eastern and international markets. Although millions of bushels of wheat and millions of barrels of flour moved over the Northern Pacific lines each year, ice at Sault Ste. Marie closed Lake Superior each winter, creating serious shipping congestion during the fall and leaving the Minneapolis millers at the mercy of the hostile Chicago railroads for part of the year. Minneapolis milling interests therefore organized and financed the Soo Line to connect the Twin Cities with Sault Ste. Marie, bypassing both Lake superior and Chicago.

All these developments redounded to the good fortunes of the Twin Cities. Whereas the state's population grew more rapidly than the Twin Cities population up to 1870, between 1870 and 1890 the Twin Cities grew at more than twice the rate of the state. By 1890 almost a fourth of the state's people lived in Minneapolis and St. Paul.

As long as trade and river transportation were dominant, St. Paul retained its premier position. By 1880 the tide had turned; Minneapolis had surpassed St. Paul by 5,500 residents. When Minnesota was but an appendage of the national economy that looked eastward more than it looked west, St. Paul was a gateway to the region and the linchpin between the new territory and the nation's heartland. As settlement expanded to the west and the region became an important producer of goods and foodstuffs, Minneapolis, with its power site and its position between St. Paul and the settlement frontier, was a better location for new enterprise.

St. Anthony Falls was the economic heart of Minneapolis throughout its early history. The Mississippi fell sixty feet in three-fourths of a mile, creating many potential power sites on the river itself. More were soon built by diverting the river into canals that started above the falls and ran parallel to the river a block or two away from it. The water could then be dropped from the canals over mill wheels into tunnels that returned it to the river below the falls. At first the falls were used for sawmilling. By 1869, there were fifteen sawmills at or near the falls that produced over 100 million board feet of lumber annually (Figure 7). After 1870 sawmilling gradually gave way to flour milling in terms of product value, but flour milling increased without diminishing sawmilling. Production increased until 1900. Even though out-

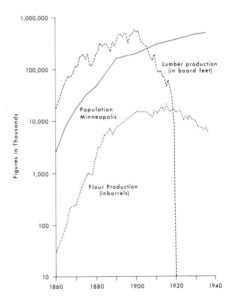

Figure 7. Growth and decline of lumbering and flour milling in Minneapolis, 1860 to 1940. Based on Calvin F. Schmid, *A Social Saga of Two Cities*, Chart 6.

put dropped somewhat thereafter, sawmilling continued to be a mainstay of the Minneapolis economy until 1915, when it declined precipitiously, the local timber having been exhausted.

Lumber milling set the stage for flour milling by generating local capital, promoting railroad construction, and stimulating employment and manufacturing. By 1870, at the beginning of the wheat boom, there were thirteen flour mills in Minneapolis that produced more than 250,000 barrels of flour annually. Up to that time they had engaged mostly in custom milling for local use. Larger scale enterprise was hampered by poor rail connections into expanding wheat areas to the west and to eastern markets. But production for export rose rapidly after 1870.

After 1880 the industry began to consolidate. Whereas the twenty mills operating in 1876 were run by seventeen different firms, by 1890 four companies owned almost nine-tenths of the city's milling capacity. C.A. Pillsbury and Company was the largest. The Washburn-Crosby Milling Company (later General Mills) ran a close second.

Thus did Minneapolis become the Mill City, yet ancillary industries provided more jobs than the mills themselves. Thousands worked in companies manufacturing bags, barrels, breakfast foods, livestock feeds, milling machinery, and vegetable oils depending directly on the milling industry. Milling dominated the city's skyline as well as its industrial structure. The mills clustered around the falls and the grain elevators that line the railroad tracks throughout Minneapolis make Mill City a sobriquet that is still appropriate even though milling's heyday ended with World War I.

Meanwhile, back in St. Paul trade, transportation, and diversified industry flourished. River transportation and the fur trade stimulated firms engaged in wholesale and retail trade and others manufacturing the goods that moved in trade. In the prerail era, shoemaking, saddlery, and other leather-fabricating trades were important offshoots of commerce in furs and hides. Although St. Paul did little sawmilling, manufactured wood products firms did flourish. Carriage building, furniture construction, garment making, and hardware manufacturing were other important enterprises in the 1860s. Up to the 1880s, St. Paul retained its lead in wholesale trade, but by 1890 Minneapolis surpassed it. No single industry came to dominate the St. Paul economy the way milling did in Minneapolis. Instead, numerous small firms that depended on St. Paul's role as a transportation and mercantile center provided jobs for St. Paul's residents.

St. Paul's earlier start and firmer financial relationships with the East made it an early banking center, and many of the Twin Cities' banking fortunes started there. Being a government center as well, the city was a favorable environment for ambitious, perceptive financiers like James J. Hill. The eighteen year old Hill had arrived in St. Paul in 1856 with a vague notion of continuing on to the Red River country. The fall wagon train had left, so he took a job as a shipping clerk with a steamboat company. He soon started his own river freight and fuel supply company, which then led him into other commercial ventures. Hill had a prescient grasp of the region's future economic geography and the degree to which the region would depend on railroad transportation. At length the 1873 financial panic provided the opportunity Hill and his backers had been waiting for and by 1878 they had bought the bonds of the bankrupt St. Paul and Pacific. After further financial maneuvers over the succeeding fifteen years, Hill gained sole control of the railroad (redesignated the Great Northern) in 1883 and pushed it through to Seattle a decade later. In 1903 Hill and J.P. Morgan acquired the Northern Pacific and the Chicago, Burlington, and Quincy railroads and proposed to merge the three systems, but were forced to divest themselves of the Northern Pacific and the Burlington by Teddy Roosevelt's trustbusters. Whether a single rail system in the northwestern United States would have been appropriate then is debatable, but the merger of the three railroads in 1972 testifies to Hill's foresight.

The railroads connected both twins to other places equally well and thus conferred no special advantage on either city, yet they were more significant in St. Paul with its earlier emphasis on transportation and related activities. By 1880, the size of St. Paul's railroad operations was evident in the city's labor force composition in the same way that milling and ancillary activities were evident in Minneapolis.

Railroad construction fostered and perpetuated much of the bickering between Minneapolis and St. Paul in the 1860s and 1870s. Left to their own petty devices, the two cities (and perhaps even visionaries like Hill) might well have used rail routes as weapons. Fortunately, local geography left the protagonists few options. Rail lines coming from the East had to follow the broad Mississippi valley. They also had no choice but to leave the valley at St. Paul. The Mississippi flows through a deep gorge between Fort Snelling and St. Anthony Falls. The gorge was too narrow for rails and it dead-ended at the falls in any case. At St. Paul, Trout Creek had carved a gentle gradient between the river and the adjacent uplands, forming an ideal rail path. Once upland, railroads proceeded on to Minneapolis, not only because of the falls and the industry concentrated around them, but also because Nicollet Island and the falls were the best places to bridge the Mississippi. Thus, geology and economics dictated that all the railroads serve both cities regardless of local chauvanists.

The necessity to build trackage, marshaling yards, passenger terminals, warehouses, and car shops in both cities has persistently influenced land use throughout the Twin Cities. Rail yards and tracks govern the location of industry, neighborhood development, and the layout of road networks. The urban problems posed by railroad networks continue. Seven of the railroads serving the Twin Cities a decade ago have now merged into two (Burlington Northern, and the Chicago and Northwestern). The consolidated lines need much less space than they did when there was extensive duplication of facilities. Thus large tracts of railroad land in the Twin Cities are now available for development, some of them at locations adjacent to the central business districts.

CONSOLIDATION, DIVERSIFICATION, AND URBAN GROWTH, 1900-1940

Minnesota's population increase approximated national growth rates after 1900, but the Twin Cities continued to gain more rapidly because of farm-to-city migration. Minneapolis lumber production peaked in 1899, declined between 1900 and 1915, and ceased four years later. The last sawmill closed in 1919. Flour milling continued to increase until 1915 but declined thereafter. After the Panama Canal opened in 1914, Pacific Northwest wheat that had formerly moved through the Twin Cities was shipped east by water. After 1922 revised railroad

tariffs made it cheaper to ship wheat to the East than to ship flour. Successful cultivation of hard winter wheat in Kansas and declining spring wheat production in Minnesota, the Dakotas, and Montana resulting from diversified argiculture combined with higher transportation costs to force Minneapolis millers to shift capacity to Buffalo and Kansas City. Flour milling products constituted over half the value of all commodities manufactured in Minneapolis in 1890. By 1930 they made up less than a fourth. As milling declined in Minneapolis it also dispersed throughout the city. Electric power made it possible to locate mills away from the falls and after 1900 mills and elevators were erected along most of the railroad trackage in Minneapolis.

As flour milling declined in favor of more diversified manufacturing in Minneapolis, St. Paul continued along the diversified lines upon which it had originally embarked. One major outgrowth of St. Paul's location and early trade was the large packing complex at South St. Paul. Meat packing was originally concentrated in St. Paul, but larger facilities were needed to process the output of the more diversified agriculture that was developing in the region. After 1900 Armour and Swift built plants and stockyards in South St. Paul that boosted the town's population from 2,000 in 1890 to 12,000 in 1940. Printing and publishing also developed into major industries during the period. Although most printing firms were small, St. Paul's printing industry was dominated by the West Publishing Company, a firm specializing in law books, and by Brown and Bigelow Co., which prints calendars and other advertising novelties.

On the eve of World War II the Twin Cities were midway in their transition from cities that made their livings by processing the region's argicultural produce to the more cosmopolitan economic centers they were to become in the postwar period when packing, milling, baking, and similar enterprises would decline. But in 1940 the Twin Cities economy was still as much related to the past as it was suggestive of the future.

The urban landscape of Minneapolis and St. Paul, on the other hand, bore slight resemblance to the two nineteenth century towns where it all began. Fifty years of growth at rates exceeding 20 percent per decade had produced a metropolis.

Swedes and Norwegians remained the largest ethnic groups in Minneapolis after 1890. Some Poles and Italians arrived after 1890, the Poles preferring Minneapolis whereas the Italians favored St. Paul. By 1910 Minneapolis had 5,000 Polish-born and 650 Italian-born, whereas St. Paul had 2,000 Italian-born and 2,000 Polish-born. The Polish-born were sometimes ethnic Poles and sometimes Polish Jews. Most of the Polish-born who went to Minneapolis were Poles, but many of the Polish-born who settled in St. Paul were Jewish.

World War I and postwar immigration restrictions combined to stabilize Twin Cities ethnic structure after 1910. In 1930 Scandinavians were dominant throughout the metropolitan region, but less important in St. Paul where the older German and Irish groups were more numerous.

Negroes and Spanish-Americans were recent arrivals in 1940. There were just under 2,000 Americans of Spanish origin in the Twin Cities then and 4,500 Negroes. Negro settlement was an offshoot of the Twin Cities rail business.

Most early Negro settlers were cooks, waiters, and sleeping car porters. Others had been brought north by the meat packers. Mexican-Americans were imported when sugar beets became an important crop in the Red River valley. Rather than make the journey to the Southwest when the harvest was over, many stayed in the Twin Cities and gradually moved into other occupations. American Indians were even less visible in 1940 then they are today. There were but 245 Indians in the Twin Cities then.

By 1940 the transition from an agrarian-based urban economy to a metropolitan manufacturing and service economy was well under way. Both cities' corporate limits were occupied except for a few tracts, and much of the neighborhood churning generated by ethnic migrations and antagonisms was over. Henceforth the Twin Cities' prosperity would depend on a new set of industries and neighborhood turnover would be more dependent on aging and lifestyle changes than on social status.

Inside the Cities

Yankee businessmen founded the Twin Cities as a moneymaking venture, attracting waves of immigrants who wanted a share of the action. The most influential group—Franklin Steele, Caleb Dorr, C.C. and W.D. Washburn, Dorilus Morrison—arrived with the vanguard of lumbermen who had started in New England and worked westward cutting over the Great Lakes forests. They were joined by other Yankee businessmen —Bassett, Pillsbury, Eastman, Welles—who were anxious to harvest the region's forests and fields and supply its residents with goods and services.

PLACES AND PEOPLE IN EARLY DAYS—JOBS FIRST, THEN HOMES

One set of jobs brought money into the area. This basic or export employment, centering on gathering raw materials, on manufacturing, and on shipping goods out of the area, concentrated at the Falls of St. Anthony, at the Nicollet Island river crossing, at the riverboat landing by the mouth of Trout Creek, and later in railroad yards and shops. Additional local service jobs served the needs of residents. These jobs concentrated in downtown centers near the intersections of major streets and horsecar lines.

The local transportation systems (streets, horsecar lines, then streetcar lines) came into contact with regionwide transportation systems (rivers, roads, railroads) in the downtown areas, making the downtowns the principal points of contact between the local economies and the rest of the world. Downtown St. Paul, on the east side of the river, enjoyed better access to

regions east and north of the Twin Cities (Figure 8). The center of St. Paul's downtown grew up west of the riverboat landing and eventually moved inland several blocks, then slowly shifted west to about Seventh and Robert Streets. Downtown Minneapolis, on the west side of the river and west of the milling district, enjoyed unrestricted access to western agricultural areas (Figure 9). Originally three downtown contenders emerged in Minneapolis and St. Anthony—Bridge Square where Washington, Hennepin, and Nicollet avenues met at the western end of the Hennepin Avenue Bridge at Nicollet Island; downtown St. Anthony at the east end of the bridge; and Lower Town on Washington Avenue near the falls . Lower Town was soon crowded out by manufacturers. Downtown St. Anthony, beleaguered by the competition, dropped from the running to become a shopping center for East (of the river) Minneapolis. Meanwhile, the commercial center of downtown Minneapolis migrated southwest toward the high class lake district, settling finally around Seventh and Nicollet.

In each city the export jobs and the downtown lay on the land like a twisted figure eight. Residential areas crowded in on every side, with the rich preempting the most scenic sites. In St. Paul, the small morainic hills directly north of downtown and Dayton's Bluff overlooking the river east of downtown became the fashionable places to live for a while, but then fashion shifted and families abruptly relocated to the bluffs at the east end of Summit Avenue where there was ample room for westward expansion. The

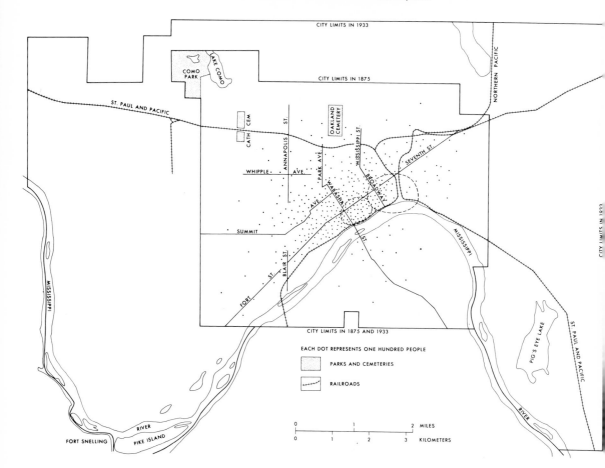

Figure 8. St. Paul in 1875. Rail lines move up Trout Creek to serve areas lying east of the Mississippi River, thereby encouraging population to grow westward from downtown. Based on Calvin F. Schmid, *A Social Saga of Two Cities*, Chart 28.

relatively flat site of early Minneapolis offered little distinctive topography as a preserve for the merchants, millers, and town fathers. Some families, including the Pillsburys, settled between the East Side milling district and the university. Others built houses on Park Avenue, which started at the falls as Cataract Street in early days and ran southward past the Washburn "Fair Oaks" estate. As time passed and the city grew, the southward-bound gold coast swung westward to Lowry Hill and the hills and lakes of Kenwood near Lake of the Isles. A few first families remained in the East Side as the newly rich joined the rush to the southwest lake district.

Before 1900, neighborhood quality generally rose with increasing distance from industry, railroad yards, and the downtown. Congestion,

high densities, and general squalor near the mills gradually gave way to lower densities, higher ground, and cleaner air farther away. At the same time that St. Paul's upper class selected the bluffs west of downtown as the place to live, they assigned to railroad and industrial uses increasing amounts of land east and north of downtown where railroads converged. The same thing happened in Minneapolis. Much East Side land and parcels along the river on the West Side were devoted to railroads and industry as the upper class moved into South and Southwest Minneapolis. The rich, having alternatives, chose to avoid the noise, soot, and odors of transportation, industry, and commerce. In addition they shrewdly avoided the congestion created by a hundred trains and over a thousand railroad cars entering and leaving the

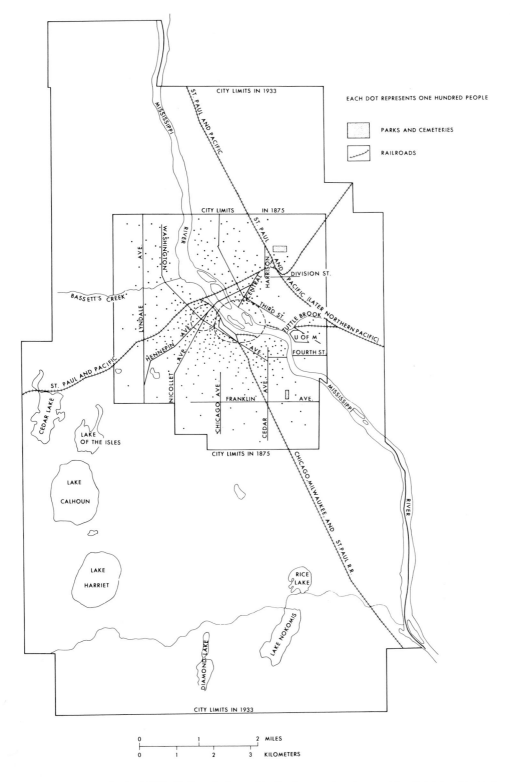

Figure 9. Minneapolis in 1875. Railroads from St. Paul cross the river at Nicollet Island just above St. Anthony Falls, then continue westward hindering easy access between downtown and North Minneapolis. Based on Calvin F. Schmid, *A Social Saga of Two Cities*, Chart 27.

cities daily, blocking streets and isolating certain neighborhoods for hours on end (Figure 10). For several decades in both cities most railroads crossed city streets at grade. South Minneapolis and western St. Paul were the only places enjoying continuous and unrestricted access to their downtowns without railroads blocking the way. So in both cities, early upper income migrations set the dominant directions of growth—Minneapolis southward and St. Paul westward—that continue to the present day.

By the turn of the century, Minneapolis community leaders—Protestant, native-born, and monopolizing finance, civic administration, trade, management, and the professions—lived south and southwest of downtown. A mixed middle class neighborhood developed in North Minneapolis beyond the railroad tracks and Bassett's Creek. Named after a Minneapolis pioneer, the creek begins on the south side of Medicine Lake in Plymouth and flows about fifteen miles to its Mississippi outlet in North Minneapolis above the Plymouth Avenue Bridge. In early days the creek wound a tortuous course through the city in a deep and rugged chasm, blocking travel from downtown

to North Minneapolis except for a few congested bridges. Northeast Minneapolis, carved into residential islands by crisscrossing railroads and strips of industrial land, attracted mainly immigrant Poles, Slovaks, Ukranians, and Italians. A middle class residential neighborhood surrounded the university. Bohemians settled south of the university on the west side of the river, and the main line, yards, and shops of the Chicago, Milwaukee, and St. Paul Railroad running southeast of downtown Minneapolis became the spine of the immigrant Swedish neighborhood.

In St. Paul the elite were well established by 1900 in the Summit Hill neighborhood west of downtown. The city's main middle class neighborhood—settled by Swedes, Germans, Norwegians, and later by large numbers of Irish—developed to the west and northwest. The East Side (east of Rice Street), carved up by railroads and industry, attracted more immigrants from Southern and Eastern Europe, in a fashion analogous to Northeast Minneapolis. The West Side, across the river from downtown, contained mixed industrial activities, the city's main Jewish settlement, and other residential neighborhoods ranging from slums on the flood

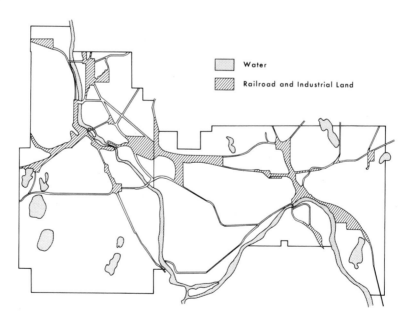

Figure 10. Railroad and industrial corridors carve up Minneapolis and St. Paul into a series of residential islands. The western part of St. Paul and South Minneapolis have been the largest parcels of uncongested land inviting continuous middle class residential development.

plain of the Mississippi to occasional elegant mansions on the high bluffs facing downtown St. Paul.

By the turn of the century the dominant immigrant groups in the Twin Cities were Swedes, Germans, and Norwegians. Poles, Russian Jews, Czechs, Slovaks, Danes, Irish, and Italians remained conspicuous but much less important. Most groups lived in all parts of both cities, but occasional concentrations were high enough to give a predominant ethnic cast to certain parts of both cities. During much of the nineteenth century the Canadian-born represented one of the largest immigrant groups, but they remained inconspicuous except for the few who spoke French.

PEOPLE TODAY

During the 1960s the European foreign stock in the Twin Cities metropolitan area declined 13 percent as death overtook the older age groups. In Minneapolis and St. Paul the decline was even higher. Each city lost about a third of its foreign stock, which dispersed to the suburbs faster than the rest of the population.

Between 1957 and 1971 the city of Minneapolis lost 60 percent of its Jewish population. In contrast with other ethnic groups, large numbers migrated en masse to a couple of suburbs while the Jewish proportion of the area population declined to 2 percent. Near North Minneapolis, which had 38 percent of the area's Jewish population in 1957, lost 94 percent of its Jewish residents during that period. By 1971 more than three out of four Minneapolis area Jews lived in the suburbs, with 48 percent living in St. Louis Park where Jews comprise 20 percent of the population.

The Jewish departure from the Minneapolis Near North left vacant many quality houses which were promptly occupied by black families. Prosperity encouraged the better-off and upwardly mobile black families to move steadily westward and northward away from the North Side ghetto core near 6th Avenue North and Lyndale. As they moved others followed, pushed along by urban renewal projects.

It is uncertain why Minneapolis developed separate black neighborhoods on the North and the South sides, but the Glenwood Avenue North–Fourth Avenue South streetcar line which ran between the two neighborhoods for three generations through downtown Minneap-

olis without a transfer stop may offer a clue. The two ghettos lay separated on the map but remained conveniently linked by a single transit line (Figure 11).

In St. Paul, Mexican and Chicano neighborhoods emerged on the West Side when former Jewish residents abandoned it for better housing across the river on Selby Avenue west of downtown and then for Highland Park southwest of downtown. St. Paul's principal black neighborhood developed at the western edge of downtown at the type of location where black neighborhoods usually develop—the inner precincts of the city's most vigorously expanding middle class residential sector.

There were over 30,000 blacks in the three sprawling ghetto neighborhoods in 1970. Each was small, integrated by ghetto standards elsewhere, and mixed in income, education, age, and occupational characteristics compared to black areas in most other large American cities.

In recent years the black minority—with a sizable number of professionals, civil servants, corporate executives, and foundation personnel—has realized steady acceptance or cooptation into Twin City economic, political, and civic life. Farther down the social ladder, the frequently shrill rhetoric of Indian and Chicano leaders reflects the distance these recent immigrants must travel toward full participation in local affairs.

CHURCHES AND SCHOOLS

Residential neighborhoods grew up around job opportunities. Inside the neighborhoods immigrant groups organized much of their life around churches and schools. The predominant Scandinavian and German origins of the population meant that Twin Cities church members have been overwhelmingly Lutheran or Roman Catholic.

Almost a third of all church members in the area are Lutheran, with the American Lutheran Church, nationally headquartered in Minneapolis, claiming the largest share. The original branches of the Lutheran Church were organized largely around ethnic congregations—Evangelical Lutheran (Norwegian), Augustana Lutheran (Swedish), American Lutheran (German), and United Evangelical Lutheran (Danish). A controversy over public education developed in Twin Cities Lutheran circles during the nineteenth century, but the immigrant press and

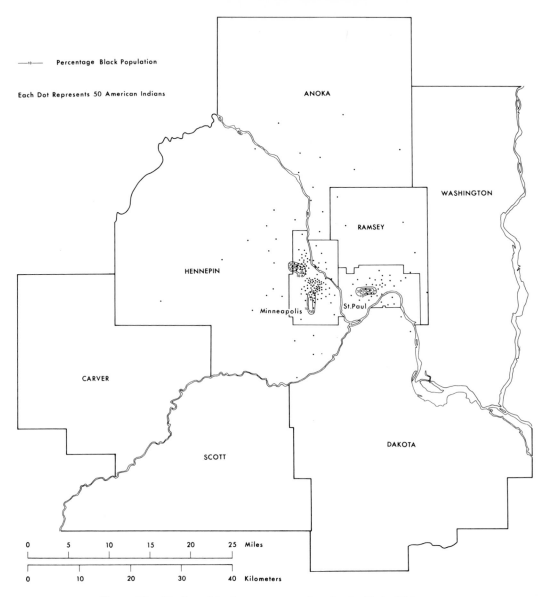

Figure 11. Black and Indian concentrations in the Twin Cities.

people generally supported the public schools and do so today.

Over 43 percent of church members in 1971 were Roman Catholic. They support an extensive system of territorial parishes serving all parts of the Twin Cities. The United States was considered missionary territory by Rome until 1908. Church authorities in Rome and in the states responded to the threat of Protestantism and the risk of leakage by creating both territorial and personal parishes. Each diocese, including the St. Paul diocese con-

taining the Twin Cities, was completely subdivided by the authority of the local bishop into nonoverlapping areal units called territorial parishes (Figure 12). In addition, national or language-based parishes were formally constituted without boundaries as "personal parishes"—e.g., Polish, Slovak, German, Lebanese—or else resulted from the bishop formally recognizing the ethnic composition of the area served by a territorial parish—e.g., German parishes west of Minneapolis—by designating it a national parish and by assigning to it parish

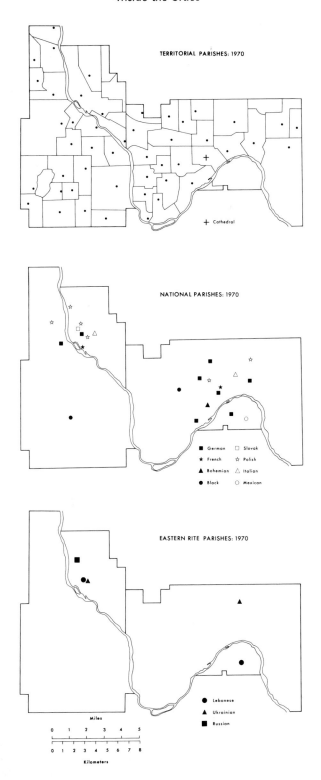

Figure 12. Catholic churches and parishes reveal part of the fabric of immigrant settlement in the Twin Cities. Maps courtesy of Dana Noonan.

priests who were members of the ethnic group and who spoke the language.

Several Catholic and Orthodox parishes of Eastern Rite—e.g., Ukranian, Byzantine, Greek —were also established in Northeast Minneapolis by Eastern Rite Catholic and Orthodox bishops headquartered outside the area. In each type of Catholic parish—territorial, personal, national, or Eastern Rite—an elementary school and occasionally a secondary school was built for the parish children as an alternative to the essentially Protestant-oriented public school system. Besides the Catholic schools, about two dozen additional parochial elementary and secondary schools operate today in the Twin Cities, mainly under Baptist and Lutheran jurisdiction. A few private nondenominational academies operate without institutional support and enroll mainly children from upper income areas.

Patterns of parochial school attendance in the Twin Cities today tell us as much about class structure as about the local geography of religion (Figure 13). The largest and strongest Catholic parochial elementary schools thrive in middle and upper middle class areas having substantial numbers of third and fourth generation Catholic families of Irish, German, and Austrian descent. In the Twin Cities this means the middle and higher income areas of South, Southwest, North, and Northeast Minneapolis, and most of the west half of St. Paul and its eastern edge. Catholic parochial schools have the hardest time surviving in lower income areas, black neighborhoods, and Indian areas, even though a substantial fraction of Indians are Catholic. A significant number of upwardly mobile black families, uncertain about the educational and social environments of the public schools and wanting something distinctive or

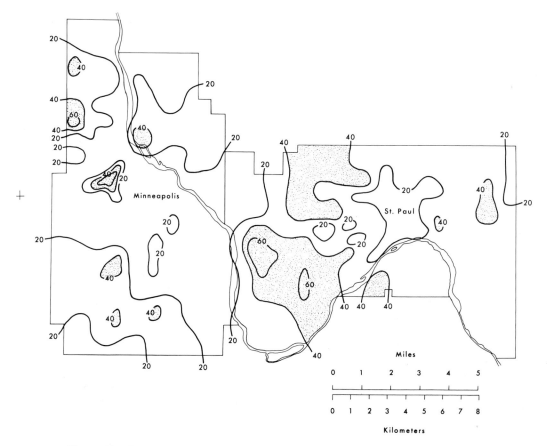

Figure 13. Percentage of elementary school children in nonpublic schools, 1970.

more exclusive for their children, send them to parochial schools. In traditionally Scandinavian middle class South Minneapolis, a number of Lutheran parochial schools enroll fair numbers of students.

Some parents elect to send their children to parochial schools for doctrinal reasons, some prefer the more exclusive atmosphere of an alternative school supervised by a neighborhood parish board of education, and others seek curricular variety. Some Twin Cities parochial schools are more progressive and others are more traditional than the public schools. Race is seldom a reason because public school attendance areas are designed to keep minority enrollments small compared to other cities (Minneapolis, 18 percent in 1973, up from 7 percent in 1963) and because many nonpublic schools enroll a significant number of minority students.

The availability of high quality alternative schools for many families, combined with the relatively high social class and small numbers of minority populations, make it hard to assess the relationships between race, class, schools, and the inclination of families with school age children to move into or out of middle class neighborhoods in either Minneapolis or St. Paul. Parochial schools thrive in such middle class neighborhoods and frequently become—with the church community around them—an important social, political, and neighborhood force attracting new families and retaining the old because of the strong community bonds, long lost in other cities but successfully maintained here.

Moreover, although the parents may hold views different from those of their children, about seven out of ten students surveyed in Minneapolis secondary schools in 1972 said they think it is a good idea for students of different races to go to school together. Some of the highest percentages of students favoring integration were recorded in the city's most integrated schools. Racial attitudes such as these suggest a positive educational picture in other areas as well. Of the public high school students surveyed, a substantial majority liked school, were good students, and were successful after graduation. On national achievement tests in English, Minneapolis eleventh graders scored 49, slightly below the national norm of 52.5. On scores of the American College Testing Program, college-bound twelfth graders earned a mean score of 20.3 in 1971-1972, doing better than their peers around the nation who averaged 18.8. The city publishes each year the records of continuing high quality of its public school students, a reflection of the willingness of middle class families to live in the city. None of the suburbs publishes its records.

Not to be outdone, St. Paul public schools reported in 1973 that student achievement levels have risen steadily since 1970 after falling each year for the previous five years. The more affluent the family, the better the student seems to do, and the city—always an attractive place for middle class families—evidently is more than holding its own in competition with the suburbs. The 1972 test scores were below 1965, before the decline started, but current results are expected to exceed those of 1965.

Almost half of the 1971 graduates of Minneapolis public high schools were attending college in 1972 and were doing well. Besides the 46 percent in college, 10 percent were enrolled in trade or technical schools, over 37 percent were employed, and 2 percent were in the armed forces.

HOUSING AND NEIGHBORHOODS

From the time of initial settlement until today the growth of the Twin Cities population has been accompanied by a steady expansion in the local housing supply. In fact, the housing inventory has increased even faster, accompanying the sharp decline in average household size in recent generations. Almost all nineteenth century houses were constructed of wood, the cheapest and locally most abundant building material. After the usual series of major fires which swept through nineteenth century midwestern cities, the cities established fire limits, zones around downtown within which only brick and stone buildings were permitted. Their durable construction meant that many of them remain in use today. Fires and the expansion of the downtowns removed most of the housing built before the 1880s.

What little remains of the pre-1890 housing was compactly clustered around the central employment and shopping cores. People and housing huddled within walking distance of downtown. During the economic and population boom of the 1880s the cities became increasingly congested. Reliance on walking, especially during winter, prevented the cities from sprawling outward. Upward expansion was normally impossible because up to the 1880s no one knew how to build economical tall buildings that would support their own weight. Moreover, even if the buildings could be built, a limit of six stories or so existed on the number of flights of stairs a person could climb without collapsing. Thus, one force pulled the cities inward, another kept them low in profile.

Cities like Minneapolis and St. Paul that grew rapidly during the late nineteenth century had only one means of dispersing houses and people, and then only for the privileged classes —the railroad suburbs of the sort found around much larger cities like New York, Boston, Philadelphia, or Chicago. Smaller places like St. Paul and Minneapolis accommodated their pre-1880 growth by cramming the poor and working classes into rather tight quarters with block after block featuring population densities that sometimes reached several hundred people per acre.

Two important inventions of the 1880s removed the constraints preventing the areal expansion of cities and encouraged lower density residential development. One was the construction of steel- and metal-frame buildings, beginning with the Chicago skyscrapers in the mid-1880s, demonstrating how cities could expand upward. Electrification of the horsecar lines and steam-propelled street railways produced the electric streetcar, permitting outward dispersal of the city and giving working class people a chance to live outside the congestion and still move quickly and cheaply to work and shopping.

The new housing during the electric streetcar era was built in neighborhoods served by streetcar lines. Most streetcar lines in Minneapolis were built to serve the South Side, reinforcing growth in that sector of town especially into the southwest lake district (Figure 14). In St. Paul, all the 1884 lines ran west or north of downtown, setting the future course of residential growth. By 1905 the cities' limits had almost reached their present extent. The transit systems of the two cities had merged on Como and on University avenues in St. Paul's Midway district, setting the stage for that area's rise in the 1920s as a major zone of manufacturing and goods handling, close to the railroads of both cities, with plenty of flat vacant land, easy to reach by streetcar from either city.

The outstanding growth of the Twin Cities during the 1870s and 1880s nurtured extravagant expectations on the part of the streetcar companies' owners and eventually they overbuilt the network to 523 miles. Perhaps taking a cue from railroad magnate James J. Hill who had made a fortune on land grants, the streetcar companies under the management of William King and Thomas Lowry also entered the land business because any land served by the streetcar could be developed for residential use and transfer points between lines were ideal commercial locations. When urban growth fell short of expectations, the surplus land was eventually soaked up by large lots, producing some of the lowest residential densities found among midwestern cities.

St. Paul streetcar lines reached South St. Paul and the stockyards, Stillwater on the St. Croix River, North St. Paul, Wildwood Park, and fashionable White Bear Lake. Minneapolis lines reached out to the towns of Robbinsdale, St. Louis Park, and Hopkins, and to the streetcar suburbs and resort areas on Lake Minnetonka. Trolley lines also connected with interurban lines to Hastings and Anoka. Like streetcar entrepreneurs in other cities, the Twin Cities company built amusement parks at the ends of the out-of-town lines to keep people riding on holidays and weekends. Wildwood Park north of St. Paul and Excelsior Park built in the 1920s on Lake Minnetonka were easily reached from either city and pulled a disproportionate amount of residential construction in these directions.

National and local housing construction rates alternatively waxed and waned with business and immigration cycles. In good times such as the years after 1900 and before World War I incomes rose, immigration increased, and the housing industry boomed. Periods of war and economic recession cut the demand and supply of new housing almost to zero.

The volume of residential construction during each building era, plus the densities permitted by the prevailing urban transportation system, controlled the amounts of land devoted to residents in the Twin Cities in each era (Figure 15). Around the downtowns only traces remain of housing from the walking and horse era (pre-1890). Downtown expansion and

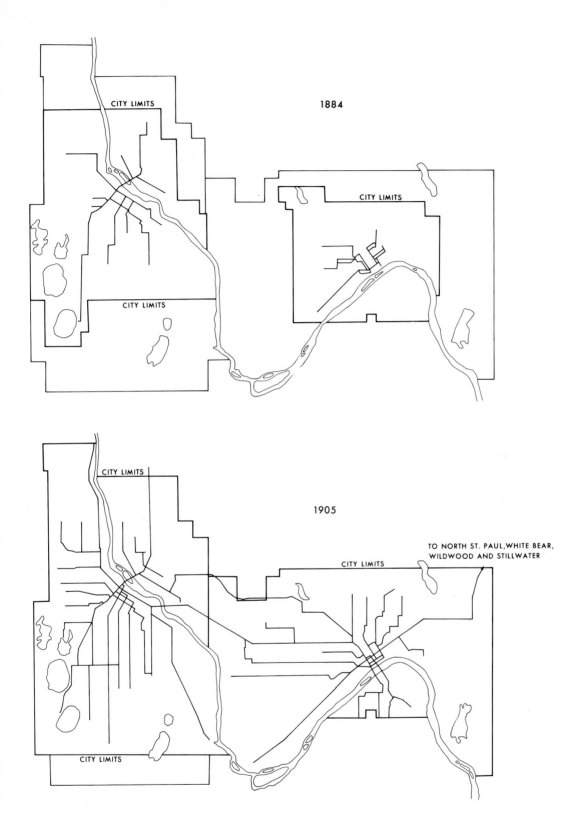

Figure 14. Expansion of the streetcar system in Minneapolis and St. Paul. Right from the start, South Minneapolis and western St. Paul were better served than other parts of the cities. Based on Calvin F. Schmid, *A Social Saga of Two Cities*, Chart 31.

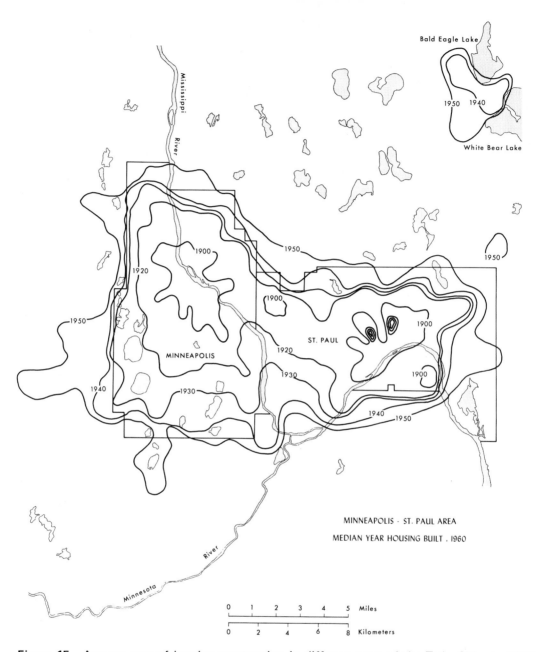

Figure 15. Average year of housing construction in different areas of the Twin Cities in 1960 reflects steady outward growth at ever lower densities. By 1970 most of the area of the map was included in the Twin Cities urbanized area. Patches of urban renewal near downtown St. Paul mean newer housing in those zones.

urban renewal took the rest. The streetcar period produced finger-shaped increments because it was easy to build outward along the lines and harder to expand between them. In the 1920s and 1930s, with cars able to move easily in every direction, a filling-in process yielded a circular-shaped city once again. Then in the postwar period highways out from the cities encouraged suburban development at the built-up margins or leap-frogged beyond.

Architectural styles and consumer tastes of each building era are reflected in each concentric increment. The boundaries between the tree-ring-like increments show up clearly. Troughs in the housing supply profile were sharp and their consequences endure. Every time the nation emerged from a serious depression or war, the cities seemed anxious to adopt new housing styles. In a boom period like the 1920s, duplexes were all the rage. Real estate was bull market, with amateur and professional investors alike thinking they could get rich quick by buying a duplex, renting half to pay for the building, and living in the other half. This scheme worked fine until too many people got into the act and owners found themselves unable to meet mortgage obligations. Yet despite the bankruptcies, the houses remain. Most of the finest duplexes in the Twin Cities represent monuments to the unflappable optimism of the 1920s.

In housing construction, when somebody does something successfully, the normal behavior pattern has been to imitate it repeatedly until a bankruptcy or a depression suggests it is time to stop. Coming out of the Depression, a different group of clients and housebuilders started with fresh styles but the behavior pattern was the same—they built only single family houses. Duplexes and apartment houses led to so many foreclosures during the 1930s that builders stuck to singles in the late 1930s and after 1945. The chronic housing shortage meant that houses could be sold as basements with roofs before they were finished. Builders assumed no one wanted anything but singles. In the mid-1960s, a few venturesome developers began building row houses and apartment houses in Twin City suburbs and discovered a strong market for them. This local experimentation was part of a nationwide trend toward greater balance in the mix of new housing styles and closer attention to household compositions and tastes. Widespread interest in mobile homes is another feature of the current housing scene. There are about 10,000 mobile homes in the Twin Cities area, with about half of them clustered north and northwest of St. Paul in southern Anoka and northern Ramsey Counties.

SHOPPING DISTRICTS AND URBAN TRANSPORTATION ERAS

Every urban transportation era modified the previous pattern of shopping districts and prompted the development of new ones. In the walking and horsecar era almost all commercial activities concentrated in the downtown cores. When streetcar tracks branched out in all directions, outlying commercial districts sprang up. Major centers featuring small department stores, doctor and dentist offices, and a wide variety of other occasional goods and services developed at the intersection of two or more streetcar lines. Other clusters of stores prospered at transit stops by supplying groceries, meat, bakery goods, pharmaceuticals, and other everyday goods and services. Ma and Pa corner stores sold bread and milk to residential areas between streetcar lines.

Farther out, in parts of the cities built up during the era of the recreational automobile, shopping districts grew up on bus and streetcar lines with provision made for car parking and, beyond the lines, at the intersections of major streets and arterials. By 1940, auto-oriented suburban shopping centers were being planned.

During the housing boom that accompanied the post-World War II freeway auto era, car-oriented shopping centers of every size and description appeared at intersections of suburban roads and highways. Shopping center developers transferred from the inner city and the streetcar era the idea of locating stores and shopping centers at traffic intersections and in strips along well-traveled streets, reasoning that if stores at such locations prospered before 1920, analogous locations farther out should work just as well after 1950. But pedestrians could move around transit intersections more easily than cars can negotiate highway intersections—and pedestrians require no parking.

Currently most of the shopping districts along transit lines are steadily going out of business. Neighborhood populations are sparser, poorer, and more mobile than they were fifty years ago. As people move outward they take their business to larger newer shopping centers. Those who remain are usually poorer than those who moved away. Sometimes the newcomers bring different tastes, such as when blacks replaced Jews on Plymouth Avenue in North Minneapolis or on Selby Avenue west of downtown St. Paul. But even the poor often have cars to carry them to larger stores and lower prices in nearby suburban shopping centers.

As retailers, dentists, doctors, and movie houses abandon the old streetcar trunk lines—

Nicollet, Broadway, Central, Lake Street, and Hennepin in Minneapolis; Seventh Street, Grand, Selby, University, Snelling, and Rice in St. Paul—the space is taken over for general office uses like insurance and real estate or by specialty goods and services like carpet and re-upholstery shops, television and electronics sales and service, pizza shops, second-hand stores, and the like. In subtle but forceful ways, new housing added on the edge draws upper income families outward and erodes the support base for central city retailers.

Downtown Minneapolis and St. Paul in contrast with other large American cities have been holding their own in retailing, but the suburban shopping centers are booming. The leading suburban shopping center developer—Dayton-Hudson Corporation—also operates the leading department store—Dayton's—in each downtown. The suburban shopping center boom started in the 1950s and by 1958 the suburbs had 11 percent of the department store trade. By 1967 it had rocketed to 52 percent.

Department store sales in Minneapolis rose from $130 million in 1958 to $143 million in 1967. Meanwhile suburban Hennepin County sales went from $23 million to $207 million. St. Paul did better than Minneapolis during the same period because of downtown rejuvenation and slower suburbanization into Ramsey County. While the Minneapolis share of department store sales dropped from 61 to 28 percent, St. Paul's share went from 28 to 21 percent. Looked at another way, Minneapolis department store sales went from $130 million to $143 million while downtown St. Paul, helped economically and psychologically by a large new Dayton's store in 1963, saw sales jump from $59 million to $107 million.

OPEN SPACE FOR THE TWIN CITIES

The Twin Cities metropolitan area, according to a study done by the Outdoor Recreation Resources Review Commission in the early 1960s, had the highest overall opportunities for participation in outdoor recreation of any metropolitan area in the country. There are two principal reasons. First is the variety of seasons. The summer is reasonable—not too hot for outdoor activities—and in the winter a continuous snow cover encourages winter sports. Second, the Twin Cities has a large amount of open space available for public use. Within the sub-urban areas there is a developing system of regional parks and a large number of lakes which are public open space (Figure 16). For weekend recreation beyond one hour's drive from home there are thousands of lakes and over ten million acres of public land. Minnesota is the third largest landowner in the United States, following only the United State government and the state of Alaska.

Serious concern for open space preservation came to the Twin Cities area with the New England pioneers who built the region. Most notably, Horace W.S. Cleveland, a gifted and original landscape architect, came to St. Paul from New England in 1872 bent on the nurturing of beauty in nature. He presented to the city council an imaginative plan for parks at Lakes Como and Phalen—still far distant from the residential centers of St. Paul. He advocated a high and commanding hill for state buildings, a splendid avenue between Minneapolis and St. Paul, and generous boulevards along the river flowing through both cities. Cleveland correctly anticipated a future growth that would make the cities physically one, scorning "artificial decorating" for a permanent "heritage of beauty." St. Paul was slow to respond, but did acquire Como Park in 1873 over the opposition of shortsighted aldermen who labeled the park as a playground for the rich who had carriages to get to it.

Minneapolis was no less lethargic at first, but when Charles M. Loring, another Maine native, became president of the newly created Board of Park Commissioners in 1883 he immediately engaged Cleveland as an aide and adviser and in two years the city purchased ten major pieces of land for parks. The city acquired the area around Minnehaha Falls and designed and constructed scenic Minnehaha Parkway linking the falls and the Minneapolis lakes. It also acquired wide strips of land around the city's five largest lakes and dredged a swamp to create Lake of the Isles (Figure 17). Many of the city's most expensive houses were built within a block or two of these lakes, particularly those to the southwest and along the Grand Rounds—an elaborate parkway system on the perimeter of three sides of the city. Most important was an arrangement with St. Paul whereby lands on both sides of the river from the university to Fort Snelling were secured for park and parkway use. Loring next launched a movement for extensive tree plant-

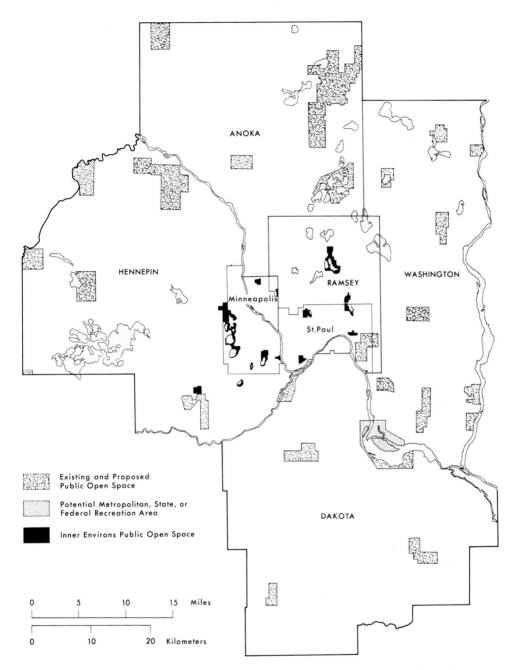

Figure 16. Recreational lakes, rivers, parks, and reserved open space in the Twin City area.

ing to shade the city streets and add beauty to travel ways. Today about the only major Twin Cities water resources remaining to be fully developed as recreational open space are stretches of the Mississippi River. Railroads and industrial uses preempted much of the riverfront in the nineteenth century. Today these uses are obsolete and should be replaced by parkland and housing. The cities, counties, and other public agencies already own much of the land along the river and pressure has begun for the governor to declare the entire stretch of Mississippi in the Twin Cities as a "critical area".

Figure 17. Lake of the Isles, just one of twenty-two lakes and lagoons in "the City of Lakes". Photo courtesy of the Minneapolis Chamber of Commerce.

The Critical Areas Act, passed by the state legislature in 1973, is designed as a permanent method for guiding development within areas of the state which possess important historic, cultural, or esthetic values and where uncontrolled development could result in irreversible damage to important natural resources. Procedurally, a "critical area" is designated by the governor upon the recommendation of the state Environmental Quality Council.

The Minneapolis city charter granted fiscal and operating autonomy to the Board of Park Commissioners. The city is divided into park districts and each district elects a commissioner to a six year term. Three other commissioners are elected at large. The board has its own taxing authority and supervises its own staff independently of the city council. St. Paul parks are managed by a department of the city government.

Besides acquiring and developing new open space, city and county park systems must maintain the health of lakes and trees. Continued urban expansion alters surface water conditions by decreasing the permeability of the ground surface and increasing the rate of runoff. Yet the lakes currently are of higher quality than the runoff. This is a serious water management problem for a region that leans so heavily on its lakes and streams. The runoff water carries increasing loads of pesticides, fertilizers, petroleum, heavy metals, construction debris, glass, salt, sulfur dioxide, and hydrocarbons. Diverting the runoff requires the pumping of Mississippi River water from above the city into the chain of lakes.

While pollution threatens the water, disease threatens many of the region's trees. Over a million stately American elms lining the boulevards and gracing the houses of Minneapolis and St. Paul will die over the next thirty to fifty years of Dutch elm disease carried by beetles who nest in the dead elm branches of live trees. The Minneapolis park board tries to replace 2 to 3 percent of its elms with different species each year as they remove dead, diseased, and damaged trees from public property. Trees on private property receive much less conscientious attention.

St. Paul and suburban areas face the same problem but cannot respond fast enough to slow the spread of the disease. Similar blights threaten red oaks and certain species of maple. The diseases spread fastest through heavy concentrations of a single species, so upper income areas with a rich variety of trees are best protected, while lower income areas with mainly elm trees for shade and decoration will be denuded first and most completely.

Suburban Open Space

Most of the large open space areas in the suburbs are county parks. Few suburban communities have done an adequate job of preserving open space or providing public park space around close-in lakes in the Minneapolis-St. Paul tradition, probably because they are too small to do it. The largest suburban park system is maintained by the Hennepin County Park Reserve District. This system contains 15,000 acres of land—almost all of it in seven large parks. Eighty percent of the land in the Hennepin system is undeveloped; the other 20 percent is utilized for picnicking, camping, nature interpretation centers, and trails. No other metropolitan counties have park systems to compare with the Hennepin system.

There is an extensive and fast-growing private open space system in the suburban areas also. Private golf courses are the most obvious part of this private open space. Private corporations such as Honeywell and 3M have built large corporate parks. There are now many planned unit developments of garden apartments and townhouses which set aside open space owned in common by residents. They also have swimming pools, ponds, garden plots, tennis courts, and picnic areas. The largest planned unit developments contain private open space areas as extensive as many large public parks.

Weekend Open Space

Most open space available for public use lies to the north of the Twin Cities in the forested part of Minnesota. About two-thirds of the forested land is in public ownership. In this forest zone, most recreational use takes place on lakeshores and to a lesser extent in managed public areas such as Itasca State Park, the Boundary Waters Canoe Area, and the Voyageurs National Park area.

Lakeshore cabins accommodate 42 percent of all the person nights spent in weekend recreation accommodations. This is twice as high as the resort percentage (20 percent) and five times as high as the camping percentage (8 percent). The heaviest concentration of lakeshore cabins is in the Brainerd area. This is where the northern pine forests and a lake area are closest to the Twin Cities. The total cabin development in this area forms the third largest built-up area in the state, exceeded only by the Twin Cities and Duluth.

TRANSIT DEVELOPMENT AND POPULATION DENSITIES

The early streetcar company, in a flush of optimism about local growth prospects, built streetcar systems for cities much larger than what eventually appeared, and started the local tradition of low density residential development. After 1920 the private car and the availability of easily developable land on every side of the built-up area promoted suburban development in many directions. Large lakes, bays, an ocean, or a wide river would have confined local growth to fewer places and kept the Twin Cities from becoming the nineteenth lowest density metropolitan area of twenty such areas in the million-plus class in the United States in 1960. Since then, densities have gone even lower.

The lethargic streetcar system never recovered from its post-World War II slump. It completed a conversion to buses in 1954 but catered only to captive ridership, neither promoting its services nor trying to compete with the car. Finally in 1967 a Metropolitan Transit Commission was created by joint agreement of many cities and soon confirmed by the legislature which subjected commission plans to the approval of the Metropolitan Council. The Transit Commission immediately began a long range transit development program starting with the 1970 acquisition of the faltering Twin City Rapid Transit Company and aiming toward an elaborate "family of vehicles" transit system built around proposed fixed guideway high capacity rail transit lines between major centers. Critics of MTC plans argue that the sprawling multi-centered Twin Cities needs no high capacity lines—especially between the centers. Instead, they argue, the area needs a vastly improved and expanded bus system and small vehicles feeding new high density residential developments proposed around the centers (the Metro Council solution), or a personal rapid transit (PRT) system providing stations within walking distance of a majority of residents and non-stop transit service on demand, moving on elevated guideways between any pair of stations. Critics of PRT argue that the perfect PRT system resembles the private car without its cost, pollutants, noise, and intrusions on nonusers. As the argument continues, the Twin Cities retains its title as the metropolitan area that has spent the most money on transit development research without building anything new. But in the long run the thoughtful and vigorous controversy will serve the area well. The one hundred mile Washington, D.C. subway system will cost over $5.5 billion or $55 million per mile. Just the annual interest on such an investment runs between $300 million (in good times) and $600 million (in bad). By way of contrast the 1974 operating revenues of the Metropolitan Transit Commission were $15 million (with a piddling operating deficit of $13 million) on total assets of $41 million and ridership of fifty-four million, and up seven million from 1972. A significant portion of this increase was accounted for by persons over sixty-five and school children who ride free during off-peak hours. The primary source of outside revenue for general operations and debt service for the Transit Commission is an *ad valorum* property tax levied upon the Metropolitan Transit Taxing District.

MTC plans call for continued bus expansion to carry seventy-eight million riders by 1985— or approximately 5 percent of the daily peak hour person trips, up from 3 percent in 1970. The current fleet of over 1,000 buses averages five years of age, compared to fifteen years when public ownership began in 1970. The buses run on 930 miles of routes, up from 521 at time of acquisition.

Besides newer buses and more routes, ridership has been augmented by aggressive advertising campaigns, direct mailings of schedules and "free ride" coupons for new routes; express service between many neighborhoods and downtowns and the university; waiting shelters; better signs and schedule information; electronic control systems; preferential bus access to freeways that meter traffic and ration car access during rush hours; and a reduction in the discriminatory charges on rides between Minneapolis and St. Paul.

While public transit has improved, it still handles a small proportion of daily person trips that are scattered over the region. Approximately 90 percent of these are as drivers or passengers in automobiles, 3 percent by bus, and 7 percent by taxis, motorcycles, and trucks for personal use. Even in the peak hours, when some highways may be congested for forty-five minutes, mass transit is used by only 6 percent of the persons making trips at this time.

Transit's role is more significant as a way of traveling to the downtown where 17 percent of the work force is employed. Transit passengers comprise 19 percent of all trips to the downtown and 22 percent of all rush hour trips (24.1 percent in Minneapolis and 19.2 percent in St. Paul). Even in these high density work areas, however, the auto is the dominant vehicle for transportation with as many people riding as passengers in cars as take the bus and twice as many driving themselves.

As the number of buses, drivers, and longer routes increase, however, the cost of operations grows more rapidly than revenues from the increased number of passengers. The operating subsidies have grown from $1 million in 1971 to $10 million in 1974 and are projected at $33 million by 1976. The consequent cost per ride was 28 cents in 1971, 70 cents in 1974, and is estimated at 85 cents in 1976. The direct public subsidy was less than 1 cent in 1971, 42 cents in 1974, and is estimated at 60 cents in 1976.

HOUSING CHOICE IN THE CITIES AND SUBURBS

Both Minneapolis and St. Paul contain an unusually wide variety of residential areas suiting assorted tastes, needs, and incomes. There is somewhat less variety in the suburbs. Lower income households find little housing there. Most of the area's inexpensive housing lies near the cores of the central cities or huddled in mobile home parks at the edges of the lower income sectors of the urbanized area. Some suburbs explicitly exclude low priced housing. An example is North Oaks at the end of Rice Street in northern Ramsey County, a former country estate owned by James J. Hill. At night barriers close off the entrances to its private streets. Only those who know the combination can push a sequence of buttons to open the gates and enter. Its 5,500 acres resemble a country club more than a residential suburb for 2,500 residents. The streets, lakes, trails, tennis courts, hockey rinks, and other facilities are privately owned and controlled by the homeowners' association to which all must belong. In 1970 the average family income exceeded $31,000, compared to about $13,000 for the average Twin Cities municipality. The average house value was over $51,000 compared to a metropolitan average of $24,000.

The mayor claims that North Oaks residents just want "a reasonable amount of privacy." Anyone who can afford up to $40,000 for a lot can move in. Building plans must be approved by an architectural committee of the homeowner's association. "We're not restrictive," says the mayor. "We just don't want some godawful deal coming in." Apartments and townhouses are prohibited under the zoning ordinances. Only single family houses on large lots are allowed. According to the planning commission chairman, the majority of the North Oaks residents have shown a "preference for perpetuation of the concepts of providing a residential area with large, rustic, residential lots in a private environment." Similar exclusive enclaves include Dellwood, Sunfish Lake, Orono, and recently developed parts of Edina and Minnetonka.

The Metropolitan Council, for its part, argues that North Oaks should provide a balanced housing supply in the community, including multifamily housing. The council worries about the areawide consequences if every suburban community prohibited the construction of low and moderately priced housing. The controversy is essentially political, centering on the desire of upper income persons to create private living spaces to their tastes, insulating themselves from poor persons and metropolitan problems by the use of municipal boundaries, versus the desire of the Metropolitan Council to ensure a choice of neighborhood and housing styles for all citizens—rich or poor. The council has forced many suburbs to make plans for publicly assisted housing as a condition for council approval when the suburbs

apply for funds from various federal park, open space, and sewer programs. The Metro Council is the area review agency that must process and approve all such applications before they go to Washington. The Metro Council recently completed a study of subsidized housing within the seven county Twin Cities metropolitan area. Housing opportunities for lower income persons are increasing slowly throughout the metropolitan area. A total of fifty-four municipalities in the region have some subsidized housing, either planned or existing.

There is a disproportionate concentration of subsidized housing in the two center cities. Minneapolis, for example, has 24 percent of the area's population and 57 percent of the area's subsidized housing. St. Paul has 17 percent of the area's population and 31 percent of the subsidized housing. The suburbs contain about 60 percent of the total population but they include only 12 percent of all federally subsidized housing. Several communities in addition to Minneapolis and St. Paul have slightly higher percentages of subsidized housing than their corresponding percentage of population. Others are approaching their share but most communities have no subsidized housing at all.

Subsidized housing programs are based on a recognition that the gap between the cost of new housing and the ability of low and moderate income people to pay for housing cannot be bridged without governmental financial assistance. Public housing is heavily concentrated in the center cities; 98 percent of all such existing units are located in Minneapolis and St. Paul. There are eighteen HRA's (housing and redevelopment authorities) within the metropolitan area and the number is gradually increasing, but many of those in suburban communities have public housing units only in the proposal stages. Most of the public housing units—70 percent of those in the two central cities; 98 percent of those in suburban and rural areas—have been built or are being planned for the elderly.

In contrast to public housing, other programs aimed primarily at moderate income people operate in Minneapolis and St. Paul. The two center cities contain 81 percent of all such new federally assisted housing. Other programs previously found in the two central cities provide mostly used housing. They include subsidized rental for leasing of housing units, spot acquisitions and subsidized loans for home ownership, and low interest loans or grants for rehabilitation of housing owned by moderate and low income persons. The state in 1973 also developed its own housing program consisting of subsidized loans for new housing and loans and grants for rehabilitation. Both Minneapolis and St. Paul in 1974 also began rehabilitation programs with funds to make loans and grants available for rehabilitation.

When suburbs put walls around their borders and keep out the poor, the aged, and many minorities, they also reduce the bite of the tax collector. In the plushest suburbs a person can build a $100,000 house and have one of the lowest tax bills in the metropolitan area since these suburbs frequently have a substantial commercial and industrial tax base to share the tax load. In 1974 the average tax on a $25,000 house was $401 or 1.60 percent of market value, down from $468 (or 1.87 percent) a year earlier. Yet the taxes on the same house from one jurisdiction to another, making allowance for variation in assessment practices, range from $273 in Inver Grove Heights to $688 in Circle Pines.

Besides disparities in tax treatment, additional disparities exist in expenditure patterns. Such fiscal disparities are a common problem in every American metropolitan area. They disrupt and damage the quality of life. When disparities in tax treatment among jurisdictions reach beyond two to one it means that a resident in the least favored community must tax himself at a rate over twice that assessed on a resident in the most favored community in order to obtain the same level of public services.

Fiscal disparity becomes a serious issue because the fiscal system that cultivates the disparity is inequitable and unfair—persons and families with the same ability to pay are taxed at different rates for the same services just because they live within one set of boundaries with higher value industrial and commercial development instead of another that lacks them. The system that creates fiscal disparities is wasteful because it encourages families and businesses to select locations for individual fiscal advantages (lower tax rates; better services) while ignoring communitywide waste of resources.

In responding to these problems the Minnesota state legislature in 1971 passed three laws—a Fiscal Disparities Act, a substantially changed school aid law, and a municipal state aid law.

The effect of these was to give taxpayers in communities with little or no new tax base from commercial and industrial development a share of the metropolitanwide increment and to provide percentage equalization in municipal and school finance so that places with low returns per mill of tax effort would get more state aid than those with high returns. Thus, each family or business should get the same returns for similar tax effort no matter which community they chose to settle in. To reduce fiscal disparities in the tax base, 40 percent of the tax base attributable to commercial and industrial *growth* in the metropolitan area since 1970 is diverted to a metropolitan equity fund and redistributed to municipalities and school districts based on their population and expenditures. The Fiscal Disparities Act does not interfere directly with the private, suburban preserves of the wealthy, nor does it speed up the production or scattering of low and moderate income housing. What it does is eliminate some of the unfairness that normally accompanies suburbanization.

Population Redistribution

In both central cities the oldest and least desirable neighborhoods today lie within a mile or two of the downtowns. One and two unit wood-frame structures on thirty-five and forty foot lots predominate. The pre-World War I houses made no provision for automobiles, so whatever amenity is provided by the stately elm trees lining the boulevards gets diluted by streets difficult to clean and maintain and clogged by old, well-used cars. Families, especially with children, move when they can to newer houses in better-maintained neighborhoods. Those with the most initiative, information, money, and skill learn how to move to something better, but in leaving they strand a worse-off group. Neighborhood deterioration is mainly a social process with physical consequences. People who move out of a neighborhood are of a higher social class than those left behind, but they usually represent a lower class in the areas they enter. The reverse is often the case in integrated neighborhoods where the black proportion is rising, yet tensions still develop. In south central Minneapolis, at the western edge of Near North Minneapolis, and beyond the western edge of the Summit-University neighborhood in St. Paul, newcomers are often young black business and professional families, with better educations and incomes than the (often elderly) white families from whom they buy their houses. Since blacks are more conspicuous than other immigrant and ethnic groups and are generally thought to be of a lower social class than whites, their entry into a previously all-white area is interpreted as a threat to the status of the neighborhood and to the status of the families living there.

In the long run, then, neighborhood stability becomes a class or status issue rather than a racial question. In order for neighborhoods to remain stable over the long run, property-owning middle class families of mixed ages must continue to want to live in them. This result will come about only when city neighborhoods can offer advantages unavailable in newer suburbs. In Minneapolis and St. Paul, most of the central neighborhoods are undesirable by contemporary Twin Cities standards. They do not attract middle income families committed to house maintenance. As the maintenance-conscious families leave these neighborhoods some homes are turned into rental units and others are sold to lower income families who lack the resources, skills, or interest in maintenance, so that the neighborhoods move even lower in social class and the quality of their day-to-day upkeep.

One of the truly distinctive features of the Twin Cities area is the stable residential areas that surround the aging core in each city. They are found on the outer periphery of Minneapolis at its northwest and northern corners and the northeast and southern corners of St. Paul. The largest and most outstanding, however, lie in two horseshoe-shaped zones opening toward the downtowns—one in South Minneapolis bounded by the West Side chain of lakes, the crosstown Minnehaha Parkway, and the East Side Mississippi River Parkway; and the other in western St. Paul from the North Side lakes west past Lake Como to St. Anthony Park, then south along the river to Highland Park, then back along the river bluffs to Summit Hill. These residential areas may be unmatched among American central cities in their combination of sheer size, beauty, access to magnificent lakes and streams, and the nonthreatening mixture of social and racial groups that vie to live in them. Almost all lake and stream frontages are public parks. Fine houses facing the lakes sell in a few days for prices well over $100,000. House prices away from the water drop sharply block by block to less than $30,000. The neighborhoods remain highly heterogeneous in their income composition, yet all the residents want to live there. Few suburbs can offer so much.

The Metropolitan Setting

The Twin Cities 1960 population distribution was modified by small losses mainly from high density central areas undergoing extensive public and private clearance and rebuilding, and by large gains mainly in the far-flung suburbs north, west, and south of Minneapolis. Middle and upper income newcomers to the area are especially attracted to the suburbs south and west of Minneapolis while an equal number of middle and lower middle income newcomers have settled north and west of Minneapolis. The result has been a slow but steady westward movement of the region's population center.

A generation ago the center of the area's population lay just in Minneapolis between the two downtowns. Today the center of the urbanized area has drifted to just southeast of downtown Minneapolis. In contrast, the center of the St. Louis, Missouri, metropolitan area migrated westward right out of the city, leaving downtown St. Louis increasingly remote from the people it should serve. In the Twin Cities, downtown Minneapolis remains close to the center of the area's population. Some of the area's most desirable residential neighborhoods —once at the edge of the built-up area—increasingly enjoy a position at the very center of the metropolitan area.

Air travelers to the Twin Cities remark on the unexpectedly large and busy Twin Cities International Airport. Upon reaching downtown Minneapolis, where they usually go first (unless they stop along the growing "strip" of hotels west of the airport on I-494), they express surprise that it is not larger, forgetting that another city of almost equal size, with its own vigorous downtown, lies just to the east. Close inspection of daily traffic flows shows that each city draws from its own well-defined commuter suburbs. Each suburb belongs to one city or the other, never to both. As a consequence, the Minneapolis portion of the region might be viewed as two-thirds of the total and St. Paul as one-third.

Recycling the Central Cities

During the past thirty years the doubling in size and population of the Twin Cities created major problems in comprehensive planning, physical development, and governance. The chaotic suburban explosion, made possible by private cars, purchasing power stored up during World War II, and extravagant tastes for large houses on spacious lots, represented an overdue reaction to depression deprivations followed by years of wartime crowding and shortages. Meanwhile, the central cities, which up to World War II had always experienced a modest rate of continuous redevelopment and steady capital investment, entered a temporary phase of net outmigration. Today the pendulum seems to be swinging cityward once again. Instead of abandonment we now see in each city a zone of steady urban redevelopment separated from suburban development by a wide intermediate zone of residential stability.

Both cities are divided into three concentric zones, each with its special redevelopment problems and prospects. At the centers lie the downtowns, surrounded by a zone of transition to residential areas. Second come the aged and usually deteriorating pre–World War I neighborhoods. The outer half of each city forms a zone of stability with attractive well-tended houses inherited from the 1920s, 1930s, and 1940s.

THREE DECADES OF RENEWAL IN MINNEAPOLIS

In 1947 Minneapolis was close to a hundred years old. The "City of Lakes" had reached a population of 500,000 and was ringed by several relatively undeveloped suburbs. The aged parts of the central city foretold of changes to come. The average house was forty years old. Nearly 23,000 families lived in substandard houses and 6,500 were overcrowded, with more than 1.5 persons per room. The city had 700 miles of oiled dirt streets handed down from horse and buggy days. The Washington Avenue skid row, one of the country's largest, was home for 3,000 persons.

The Minnesota state legislature passed the Housing and Redevelopment Act in March 1947, to enable cities to respond to their postwar renewal needs. Later that same year Minneapolis established a Housing and Redevelopment Authority.

By the mid-1950s renewal plans for Gateway Center, the nation's most ambitious downtown redevelopment project when it began, were being completed. The depressing drain of the 1950s when Minneapolis lost 60,000 persons in the productive fifteen to sixty-four age group while gaining 16,000 elderly and 14,000 dependent children, soon gave way to the boom of the 1960s. The Guthrie Theatre was formed, four major league sports arrived, the metropolitan airport was rebuilt and expanded, the metropolitan freeway system was laid out and built, the University of Minnesota grew to over 40,000 students, and economic expansion promised renewed vitality for the second century of Minneapolis.

Gateway Center has now replaced skid row, forming part of a quarter-billion dollar private investment in downtown Minneapolis. For the first time in fifty years new housing was built in the heart of the city. The Towers Apartments and Condominiums contain 500 units. Additional private high-rise apartments and high-rise public housing for the elderly bring the total close to 2,000 new units.

The Nicollet Mall provides a pedestrian spine linking Gateway Center to the heart of the retail district (Figure 18). The tree-lined mall is reserved for pedestrians and buses only. A large reflecting pool and sculptered sand garden at Minoru Yamasaki's Northwestern National Life building decorate the north end of the Mall. Completing the downtown redevelopment is a pedestrian walkway system linking over twenty downtown blocks by second story sky-ways over the streets (Figure 19). Most businesses and residents consider the downtown redevelopment to be an unqualified success.

The core of downtown Minneapolis is divided into a medium density (B4-1) zone and a high density (B4-2) zone. Surface parking surrounds the core. The reason for high density core and vacant periphery is economics and the city zoning code. The zoning code has a vastly higher parking requirement for developments outside the core. In the medium density zone no parking is required until the development reaches 400,000 square feet and in the high density zone no parking until the 800,000 square feet level is reached. Outside the core, parking must be provided at a rate of

Figure 18. Nicollet Mall in downtown Minneapolis. Photo courtesy of the Minneapolis Chamber of Commerce.

Figure 19. The climate-controlled Minneapolis skyway system unifies the heart of downtown and separates pedestrian and vehicular movement. Photo courtesy of the Minneapolis Chamber of Commerce.

one space for each 300 square feet of building space over the first 400,000 square feet. Therefore, a 400,000 square foot structure in the high density zone requires no parking, whereas outside that zone parking for 1,320 cars would be required (the Northstar Ramp, downtown's largest, holds 986 cars). Needless to say, this parking requirement acts as a severe constraint to any development outside the core. The only major development to occur outside this core zone has been the Northwestern National Life Insurance building at the north end of the Nicollet Mall at Nicollet and Washington. In order to build the company had to buy from the Housing and Redevelopment Authority a whole block separate from their building at Hennepin and Second Street North so that they could meet their parking requirement. This lot was then locked into parking and cannot be changed to another use.

This high parking requirement has been both helpful and harmful. On the plus side, it has confined new developments to the core area, facilitating interchange between office and retail functions. The pinnacle of this development is the IDS (Investors Diversified Services) Center at Seventh Street and Nicollet Avenue. The clustering of buildings has resulted in the economic feasibility of employing skyways that are primarily financed and built to connect the intensely used core at the second floor levels (Figure 20). Planners feel the skyway system once installed now tends to cluster development in the core because a skyway link to the rest of the system makes a new development much more financially sound.

Because this parking requirement has worked so well to build a compact retail-office core, it has left many vacant parcels of land around its periphery. Another reason for the vacant lots is that a higher return is to be had from surface parking than from marginal, old-

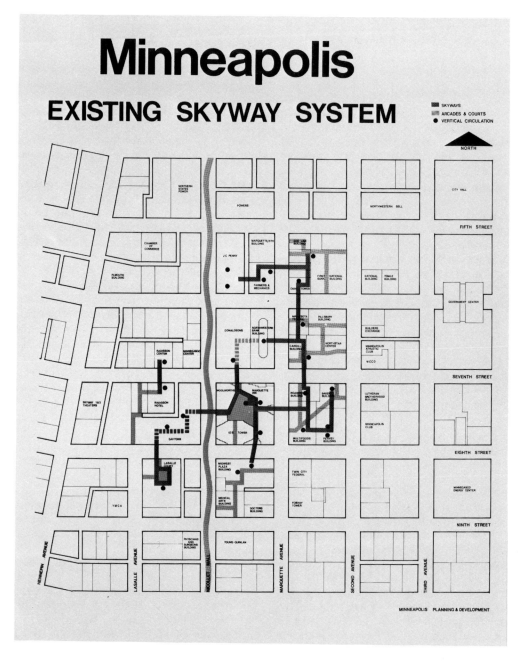

Figure 20. The existing skyway system in downtown Minneapolis. Photo courtesy of the Minneapolis Chamber of Commerce.

er buildings—especially warehouses, loft buildings, obsolete hotels, apartments, and small stores and shops that once served nearby residences. Careful downtown planning has encouraged a compact retail-office center and provided a land bank for expansion of this center. Yet promoting core development has meant hindering progress in the Gateway urban renewal project area. About one-third of the remaining Gateway area land has been designated for office-commercial use. This land seems to be just a few blocks too far away from the core.

Thus the existing downtown pattern is changing. The demand for new private office space over the next few years will require sites that currently lie outside the core or in redeveloped portions of the core. The city of Minneapolis and businessmen's Downtown Council have agreed that all-day parking should be restricted in the core and moved to the periphery of the CBD. Major new office buildings such as the IDS Center were limited in the number of parking spaces they could provide on their site. A revised zoning code will expand the core's B4-1 and B4-2 districts out about one and one-half blocks. The expansion will not only encourage building without provision of parking, but will actually limit the maximum number of spaces that can be built in a particular block. Along with this zoning change, the city will be building municipal parking ramps around the periphery of this CBD to accommodate all-day parking. Commuters will move from ramps to the core on minibuses and through extensions of the skyways.

URBAN RENEWAL AND PUBLIC HOUSING IN ST. PAUL

St. Paul's public renewal programs began with the Federal Urban Renewal Law of 1949. The Housing Authority has since undertaken several federally aided projects. Others began under the Port Authority which is authorized by the legislature to manage and develop river port facilities and its extensive land holdings along the river. The State Capitol Approach Area redevelopment was launched under the State Veteran Service Building Commission. In addition, a large public housing program built over 3,000 units.

Like Minneapolis, the initial emphasis was on redevelopment in which the worst nineteenth century slum areas were replaced by new and different uses. By now the major blighted areas are gone and emphasis has moved to rehabilitation and conservation—retaining the basic character of communities and neighborhoods but updating the physical plant.

Interest in downtown redevelopment began with a plan by Victor Gruen's firm commissioned in 1958 by a group of St. Paul businessmen. The popular plan failed to materialize when the highway department declined to reroute Interstate 94 to north of the capitol, but the Housing and Redevelopment Authority responded soon with other plans, encouraged by support from the Chamber of Commerce and the Metropolitan Improvement Committee, a group of labor leaders, professionals, and business persons organized to promote citywide renewal and improvement especially for commercial uses. In 1962 the planning board approved the twelve block, forty-three acre Capital Centre renewal project in the heart of downtown. All but a few of the structures had been built before 1920 and most were replaced.

Now that the redevelopment is largely complete, one cluster of blocks is mainly in retail use, commercial and office uses fill another area, and residential areas lie along a zone facing southward toward the river. A skyway system built as part of the public renewal program links more than ten blocks downtown, and plans are underway for a five block tree-lined mall with benches, fountains, and lanes for buses. Sidewalks would be widened to seventeen feet. Financing, like that for the Nicollet Mall, would come from assessments against benefiting merchants and perhaps from federal transit funds.

The new project cost of most past urban renewal activities in St. Paul was financed two-thirds by the federal government and one-third by the city. In Capital Centre, the federal government paid three-fourths of the project costs and St. Paul paid one-fourth plus administrative costs. The city's payments were in cash or credit for noncash grants-in-aid (property improvements such as streets, sewers, lighting, etc. made in the project). The tax receipts from Capital Centre before urban renewal began in 1964 amounted to $710,000 annually. Upon completion, the tax return in the project is estimated to be $2,500,000.

The housing authorities in Minneapolis and in St. Paul have been run vigorously, intelligently, and sensitively, especially in recent years, but a debate continues whether neigh-borhood rehabilitation efforts will be sufficient to create and maintain stable residential and commercial areas within the low income sec-tions of the cities.

The controversy centers partly on whether the poor should be given a wider choice of dis-persed housing opportunities. The South High nonprofit housing project at Cedar Avenue and East 24th Street in Minneapolis is a 212 unit Indian-inspired housing community, the first such project planned and completed by urban Indians anywhere in the country. The residents, almost 40 percent of them Indian, have a gov-erning council of twenty-five who set policy and approve new plans such as a ninety child day care center to be housed in the commu-nity center. It is doubtful that an effort to disperse this community would find many sup-porters.

CAN THE VITALITY BE SUSTAINED?

Like most American cities, Minneapolis and St. Paul came out of World War II with cluttered downtown centers, ragged legacies from the 1920s. Suburbs were booming and downtown abandonment seemed imminent. From today's vantage point we see that reports of the death of the downtowns were greatly exaggerated. Across the country, downtowns were redesigned and rebuilt, some quickly and some only after long delays.

Minneapolis began a steady remodeling of its downtown with the Gateway redevelopment in the early 1950s. The rest of the retail and commercial portion of downtown has been con-fidently rebuilding ever since. The St. Paul re-development effort started later, but once begun with the Capitol Approach, Eastern, and West-ern redevelopments, spilled into the center of downtown and continues briskly today.

The Twin Cities downtowns are not Atlanta, whose mile-and-a-half business strip along Peachtree Street sports a unified concentration of new office towers, hotels, shopping facilities, landscaped streets, plazas, parks—and a $700 million price tag. Yet certain city-building principles of the 1960s and 1970s remain the same in both places. It all starts with a visionary and somewhat incestuous coalition of business and civic officials who promote bold plans, massive investment of private and public capi-tal, and high standards of coherent urban design

to nurture an image at home and inspire the confidence of investors elsewhere. Meanwhile, the massive expenditure of hundreds of mil-lions of redevelopment dollars is recycled and multiplied within the local economy, helping to produce the vitality investors seek to exploit and triggering additional votes of confidence and further waves of investment. The forecasts become self-fulfilling. The redevelopment busi-ness is itself a big business. Stretched out for a long enough time the redevelopment of down-towns can grubstake a sizable chunk of a local economy for an entire generation.

Despite the fanfare and sparkling new im-ages, downtown redevelopments along with debt-financed urban development in general has its critics. "Nicollet Maul" reads the index item for the downtown Minneapolis shopping street in the fourth annual report of the federal Council on Environmental Quality. A typo-graphical error, of course, but capturing well the flavor of the report's comments. The mall was described as "[a] pleasant shopping ex-perience with the feel of the city and the com-fort of a suburban mall," but the area around the mall got bad reviews. The report is critical of cities—Minneapolis and Atlanta cited as examples—that are losing or have lost a balance between new high-rise buildings and older, smaller ones, and producing a "bombed out" look in many downtowns. In both Minneapolis and Atlanta, the report continues, the down-town commercial core has developed into a strip little more than a block wide surrounded by acres of parking lots, creating an environ-ment hostile to pedestrians a few steps off Peachtree Street or Nicollet Mall.

Public improvements and urban redevelop-ment require a continuous stream of private and public investment. In recent years the pub-lic portion has come from public borrowing and the day of reckoning is fast approaching when the payments must be made. By 1971 the governments and public service boards in the Twin City area in their various capital im-provement programs had raised their bonded indebtedness to over $1.4 billion, excluding bonds issued for public services such as water or airports to be repaid from user fees.

Since bonded indebtedness has risen much faster than either the population or the prop-erty tax base, some observers wonder whether the appearances of prosperity reflect genuine prospects for long term vitality. The outstand-ing local government debt per capita in the

Twin City area was $67 in 1950. By 1960 it almost quadrupled to $256. It rocketed to $529 per capita in 1969, then rose 13 percent more in two years to $598 in 1971. Like the extravagant fixed income household that buys and enjoys a new car or house, a sober day of reckoning eventually arrives when the bills must be paid. The Twin Cities experience is not unusual. Since 1960 per capita state and local government expenditures and debt levels have risen much faster than those at the federal level. Moreover, local governments lack convenient sources of revenue to repay their debts. The federal and state personal income tax schedules are structured so that as incomes rise the proportion that is siphoned off as taxes rises even faster—and automatically. Local governments rely heavily on property tax taxes which rise only from new development or by raising assessment levels or mill levies—both politically unpopular.

The fiscal facts raise questions whether the Twin Cities area, or any other major urban region, can continue making a major business of rebuilding itself. Much of the current rebuilding may be just the lengthened shadow of huge debt-financed capital improvements packed into a short span of years.

The Suburbs and Beyond

Surrounding the redeveloping cores and distinctive neighborhoods of the central cities, the ring of suburban development thins outward and merges into the open countryside ten to twenty miles from either the St. Paul or the Minneapolis central business district. Beyond that, for another thirty to eighty miles, branch plants and corporate administrative offices, part time farmers and long distance commuters subtly tie the small towns and countryside into the circulation network of the metropolis—the daily urban system.

THE RESIDENTIAL EXPLOSION— 1946 THROUGH THE 1950S

The legacy from the first fifteen years of postwar development is largely a residential landscape, reflecting capital poured into meeting the most obvious and immediate need—housing. The demand was spurred by four years of soldiers' dreams, the end of war time restrictions, and the need to compensate for the sluggish housing construction during the preceding decade of economic depression (Figure 21). As late as 1955 residential construction accounted for 80 percent of the value of all building permits in the principal developing suburbs of the Twin Cities. Minimal neighborhood commercial services had to be provided and, as an avalanche of youngsters reached school age, classrooms had to be built. Those developments accounted for the scant 20 percent of suburban building permit value which was nonresidential in 1955.

Single family dwellings comprised virtually all of the residential units until the late 1950s (Figure 22). It is well understood that the low mortgage interest rates and loan guarantees provided under federal housing and veterans benefit programs, as well as property tax reductions for owner-occupied homes and income tax deductions on mortgage interest, were major factors explaining the overwhelming preference for single family houses. But there was much reinforcement from other directions. Soldiers had spent a large amount of time dreaming of home; and for those from the Twin Cities and the Upper Midwest home had been an owner-occupied single family house in more than three-fourths of the cases. Furthermore, on PX juke boxes and barracks radios the most popular singers of the time had repeatedly crooned their romantic intentions to settle down at the war's end in some kind of little palace in Dallas or the San Fernando Valley—easily translated to St. Louis Park, Richfield, or Golden Valley.

So early postwar suburbia emerged. Embryonic commercial clusters and explosive expansions of former country school houses appeared at intersections on the skeleton of paved highways beyond the cities' edge. Meanwhile, building on that skeleton, landowners and small developers collectively pushed nearly 2,000 miles of new streets—usually dirt or gravel, sometimes paved—over the pastures and fields and through the woodland and divided the open areas into nearly 200,000 new lots by 1956. At the same time, hundreds of small

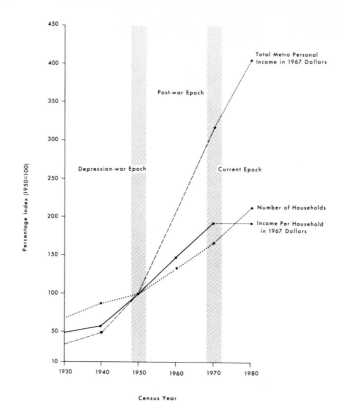

Figure 21. Changing relationships between total personal income, number of households, and income per household in the Twin Cities metropolitan area suggest that a unique post-World War II epoch has ended. Data from U.S. Census.

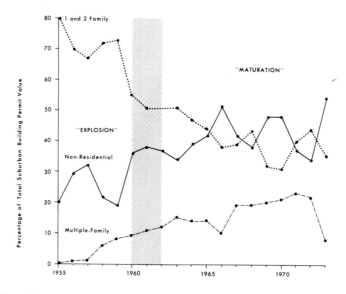

Figure 22. Residential construction in the Twin Cities by type of structure, since World War II. Changing relationships between single family, multiple family, and nonresidential construction in the suburbs suggest distinct periods of residential explosion and maturation of development within the postwar epoch. Data from the Federal Reserve Bank of Minneapolis.

builders erected new houses. Most of the builders had only one, two, or three crews and built perhaps a half dozen to twenty homes in a year. Living space in the average house was less than 1,000 square feet at first, gradually rising to about 1,200 by the mid-1950s. Soon the homes were occupied. Swarms of little children played in the raw streets, on the patches of yet undeveloped but abandoned farmland, around the edges of the ponds and marshes that were never far away. On a quiet summer evening tricycles and toys lay, abandoned for the night, helter-skelter on raw dirt yards. Inside, lights burned late in many homes while young couples taped drywalls, installed cupboards, or painted rooms. Homemade street signs, put up here and there by local residents, substituted for permanent markers which village councils—often still rural-oriented and overwhelmed by new issues —had not yet installed.

Location of New Homes

That was the metropolitan frontier. It advanced relentlessly through those years of residential explosion to enclose one hundred net new square miles of low density subdivision and another eighty-five square miles of medium and high density subdivision by 1956 (Figure 23). Behind the advancing residential frontier, lawns, shrubs, completed houses, and pavement gradually began to soften and order the raw landscape.

The location of new development during this period of residential explosion was constrained by three factors. The most important factor was the existing development pattern and circulation network; others were the organization of the building industry and housing site preferences based on past experience.

At the outset of the postwar boom, virtually all jobs in the metropolitan area were located within the central cities. At the same time most of the land available for expansion of the housing stock lay outside. There was no planned new and different program of development for the transportation and utility system. Hence the pattern of residential expansion had to follow the existing circulation network which joined potential suburban neighborhoods with the central cities. Those facilities were limited. The road grid was as dense as it is anywhere in the midwestern countryside—section line roads and many on the half-section lines. But most were gravel or graded dirt, as they had

been in the 1920s and earlier pioneer times of the automobile. There had been little improvement of rural feeder roads during the Depression and the war years. The web of paved roads in the rural periphery of the Twin Cities was thin. Hence the total network, though dense, was comparatively slow, low capacity, and low quality.

The highest development of paved roads followed five historic spokes of scattered suburban growth. The largest and most important spoke pointed westward from Minneapolis to the hilly, wooded, deeply indented shores of Lake Minnetonka. Another pointed northeastward from St. Paul to the historic attraction of White Bear Lake. A third extended southeast from St. Paul through the long-established railroad-industrial belt along the polluted reach of the Mississippi below the central cities. One more followed flat land southward from Minneapolis through an area of truck farms to the bluffs overlooking the deeply entrenched valley of the Minnesota River. The fifth and least developed followed the rail-industrial zone along the Mississippi above Minneapolis—the route of three of the five major railroads to the northwest.

The spokes along the upper and lower river were the routes of interurban streetcar lines. The Minnetonka and White Bear spokes had been served and reinforced by both suburban rail and interurban trolley lines. A few brittle remnants of the rail era system were still operating at the time the post–World War II boom began—streetcar lines as far west as Hopkins on the old route to Lake Minnetonka, to White Bear Lake, and along the lower river industrial belt beyond the stockyards and packing plants at South St. Paul. Although these lines were still considered important by some, they were ignored by the new suburbanites.

Public sewer or water systems—seldom both in one community—were confined to a handful of small streetcar suburbs—Robbinsdale in the northwest, St. Louis Park and Edina in the west, South St. Paul and North St. Paul on the southeast and northeast. Hence high density development, requiring central sewer and water, was attracted to the periphery of those suburbs or the edges of the central cities. Where houses were built at high density with dependence on individual wells and cesspools, serious problems of sewage accumulation and polluted wells followed within a few years. Notable cases

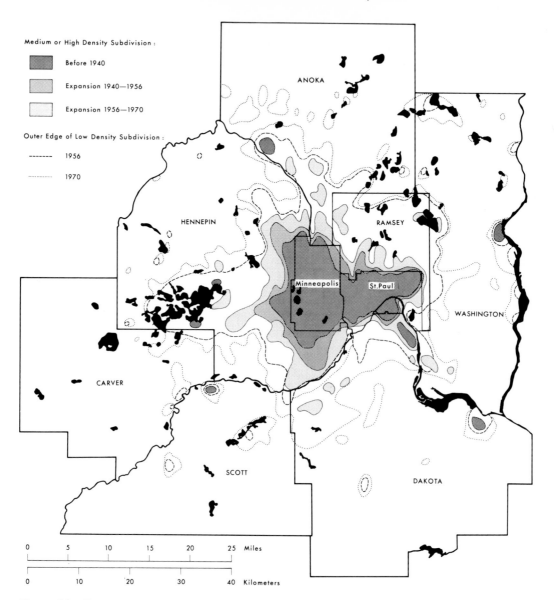

Figure 23. Extension of the built-up Twin City area after World War II. More than 300 square miles of low density subdivision surrounded the prewar medium and high density metropolitan core by 1956. Postwar medium and high density expansion filled in only a fraction of that vast area—forty square miles up to 1956 and another one hundred square miles from 1956 to 1970.

were in Richfield and the eastern part of Bloomington.

The tendency to stick close to existing developments and transportation lines was reinforced by the character of the Twin Cities building industry. Because most housing was built by hundreds of small builders, and there were no really large developers by national

comparison, there were no comprehensively planned new towns such as Park Forest, Illinois, nor anything comparable to the Levittowns, significantly isolated from the main urban mass, beyond the position of the advancing frontier at that time. At the same time, many individual "frontiersmen" and some small builders put up single houses or small clusters on widely scattered, isolated sites in the outer part of the low density zone. That kind of settler has historically consituted about 10 percent of the Twin Cities population and probably also reflects the long-standing decentralization of the building industry and its financing.

Traditional housing site preferences also played an important role in setting the pattern of the postwar residential explosion. In some ways, they influenced the pattern at the broad metropolitan scale. The few large developers of tract housing stayed strictly with the flat glacial outwash plains. There, even in the era of the bulldozer and cheap portable drilling rig, the level surface and sandy soil enabled them to shave a little from the cost of land preparation and utilities. Hence, in the landscape created during that period, as in the older landscapes within Minneapolis, there is a vivid regionalism of more modest and homogeneous housing on the outwash plains and more expensive housing on the rolling morainic uplands.

Perhaps even more interesting is the detail of local differentiation—often from block to block or within blocks—associated with details of the glacial terrain. There are obvious strong preferences for the shores of lakes and ponds, the sides and tops of knobs on the morainic ridges, distinctive groves of birch or conifers or maples or oaks, and creeksides. And in the intricate, disorderly landscape of glacial deposition, these preferences have produced a mixture of housing —and related socioeconomic characteristics whose detail and randomness is at first hard to comprehend for most visitors from most other large American cities. This feature of residential development is probably more pronounced in the early postwar suburbs than it was in the central cities, because even early postwar suburb development was beginning to reflect the new freedom of the automobile era, to be less tied to the flat outwash plains, and to venture more into the hummocky, disordered moraine lands. But the impact of these individual preferences became much more pronounced in the 1960s.

In short, the early postwar residential boom extended and widened the five historic spokes of growth that began in the nineteenth century. High and medium density subdivision expanded mainly north, south, and southwest from Minneapolis on flat, sandy outwash plains, into Brooklyn Center, Crystal, Richfield, east-

ern Bloomington, St. Louis Park, and Hopkins. Development in those areas brought modest housing for middle income families. The principal expansion of medium density subdivision on the rougher glacial moraine land occurred between the spokes, mainly to the southwest of Minneapolis in Edina, with smaller increments west of Minneapolis in Golden Valley and north of the St. Paul Midway in Roseville. Advance of the medium density frontier was slower on the rolling moraine than on the flat outwash plains. The pioneers on the moraine were more likely to be upper middle income and to build larger than average houses on lots ranging in size from one-third to one-half acre. The low density frontier advanced much more rapidly than the medium and high. Though it retained the same spokelike configuration, more of the new growth occurred on moraine land simply because of the greater attenuation toward the big morainic lakes, especially Lake Minnetonka.

Location of New Jobs

Job growth in the suburbs lagged far behind residential growth until the middle or late 1950s. This is reflected in the lag in new building permits for nonresidential purposes. In addition to neighborhood convenience goods and service, many building materials and supply businesses mushroomed in many places, and the vanguard of warehouses and manufacturing firms began to move out from cramped quarters in obsolete multistoried buildings in the central business district of either Minneapolis or St. Paul. The companies shifting at that time were mainly those which had been most affected by the booms in housing and family formation—grocery and appliance distributors, millwork manufacturers and distributors.

The location of initial suburban job growth reflected mainly two factors (Figure 24). For one thing, concentrations of retailing and services followed the old arterials from the city into the former countryside. They represented persistence of the commercial strip idea, nourished in the streetcar era, from the central cities into the suburbs. On the face of it, strip development seemed to have little if any functional value in the new, postwar epoch. The sidewalks of the arterial streets were no longer strung out "depot platforms," where everyone who moved about the city congregated in the process of transferring from vehicle to foot or

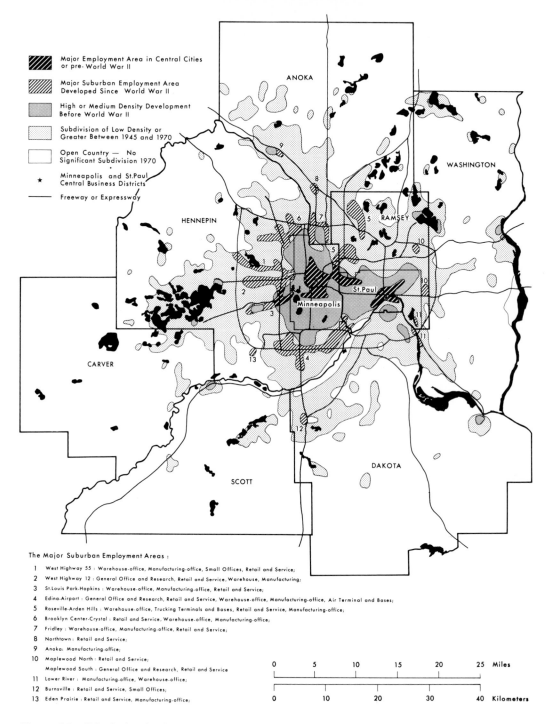

The Major Suburban Employment Areas:

1   West Highway 55 : Warehouse-office, Manufacturing-office, Small Offices, Retail and Service;

2   West Highway 12 : General Office and Research, Retail and Service, Warehouse, Manufacturing;

3   St.Louis Park-Hopkins : Warehouse-office, Manufacturing-office, Retail and Service;

4   Edina-Airport : General Office and Research, Retail and Service, Warehouse-office, Manufacturing-office, Air Terminal and Bases;

5   Roseville-Arden Hills : Warehouse-office, Trucking Terminals and Bases, Retail and Service, Manufacturing-office;

6   Brooklyn Center-Crystal : Retail and Service, Warehouse-office, Manufacturing-office;

7   Fridley : Warehouse-office, Manufacturing-office, Retail and Service;

8   Northtown : Retail and Service;

9   Anoka: Manufacturing-office;

10 Maplewood North : Retail and Service;
    Maplewood South : General Office and Research, Retail and Service

11 Lower River : Manufacturing-office, Warehouse-office;

12 Burnsville : Retail and Service, Small Offices;

13 Eden Prairie : Retail and Service, Manufacturing-office;

Figure 24. Principal suburban employment concentrations developed during the postwar epoch, mostly after 1956, and principal employment concentrations in the central cities.

foot to vehicle. In fact, the suburban arterials generally did not even have sidewalks. On the contrary, the new suburban commercial establishments hugging these streets faced virtually no pedestrian traffic, left too little room for parking, and ignored the popular suburban amenities of landscaping and open space. But perhaps there was less freedom to change the pattern at first than there appeared to be. For any business serving a regional clientele faced the question of how his customers would be able to find him. Geographical ignorance was a real problem. The names of a few arterials were well known. They conjured images of landmarks and locations. This was especially true of those which were suburban extensions of well-known Minneapolis and St. Paul commercial strips—Lake Street and Excelsior Boulevard into St. Louis Park and Hopkins, Nicollet and Lyndale avenues southward into Richfield and Bloomington, South Robert Street into West St. Paul, or Central Avenue into Columbia Heights and Fridley, for example.

The principal concentrations of industry were extensions of older rail-industrial strips. The prime example was the extension of the belt along the Millwaukee Railroad adjoining the Lake Street commercial strip from South Minneapolis into St. Louis Park and Hopkins. The origins of the St. Louis Park-Hopkins rail-industry strip go back to the nineteenth century. But it was the scene of rapid and extensive development of new food warehouses and processors and machine industries, mostly transfers from central Minneapolis during the early postwar years. Other agricultural processors and machinery or metal works expanded into the suburban reaches of the North Minneapolis upper river rail-industry strip. And a new generation of "dirty" industries—oil refining and petrochemicals which came mainly with the opening of pipelines from the new Alberta oil fields—extended the lower river rail-industry strip downstream from South St. Paul's packing plants and stockyards.

MATURATION IN THE 1960S AND 1970S

Conditions changed greatly as the years of residential explosion advanced into the late 1950s. The pent-up housing demand from the war and the Depression had been relieved. A vast new market had emerged in the suburbs and it had now become obvious to the leaders of retailing and the service businesses. Also, a vast new real property tax base had accumulated and was continuing to grow and that was obvious to the new generation of elected officials and village administrators who had moved onto the suburban political stage. Meanwhile, the suburbs of the Twin Cities, like those all across the nation, were centers of action as America moved to record high levels of personal income and buying power on which to base the financing of large scale development projects. *The Exploding Metropolis* was replaced by *The Affluent Society* as the popular reading of the time.

New Trends

New trends in suburban development accompanied these changing conditions. There was a shift toward a broader mix of housing types. Apartments, townhouses, and planned unit developments broke the virtual monopoly of the single family dwelling. The apartments and townhouses, as well as a substantial part of the new single family home construction, were located well behind the low density frontier of metropolitan growth. They served to fill in areas closer to the central cities that had been initially developed in scattered tracts at low density. Low density suburban tracts shifted to medium or high density at the rate of about three square miles per year from 1945 through 1956. From 1957 through 1970 the comparable rate was seven square miles per year. The fill-in rate more than doubled. In the latter part of the period, the Twin Cities also saw the emergence of organized innovation in the housing industry, stimulated by higher costs and growing restlessness in the market. So far these innovations have included large, planned communities of factory-assembled homes; cluster development of both single family and multiple units to preserve open space and natural amenities; and the marketing of modular and precut homes.

Meanwhile, suburban job growth began to catch up with population growth. The value of nonresidential building permits in the suburbs leveled out at 40 to 50 percent of the total. That level reflected a succession of new developments—large scale retail shopping malls, industrial parks, office parks, hospitals, high schools, regional community colleges—each a major source of suburban employment. Also, for the first time since early in the century, there was a resurgence of concern about acquiring public open space. There were major acquisitions of parkland when the frontier of development approached the boundaries of the central cities, and again in the latter part of the post–World War II building boom. Both occasions were preceded by periods of rapid residential expansion and relative neglect of public land acquisition. Behind the frontier of urbanization, municipalities bought small remaining parcels and developed them as neighborhood playgrounds. Just ahead of the advancing frontier, county and regional agencies bought tracts of hundreds or thousands of acres for regional parks, nature preservation, public golf courses, and a metropolitan zoo.

At the same time, local governments began to use their vastly increased revenue and bonding capacity to embark on public works programs that had been neglected during the frenetic years of the residential building boom. Street paving, curbing, sewer and water lines, libraries, and civic centers began to transform the suburban landscape and, incidentally, to give institutional substance to the suburban municipal governments. Some of those investments formed an important part of the greatly increased value of nonresidential building permits in the late 1950s and 1960s. While the total annual value of nonresidential building permits in the suburbs grew from typically $60 to $100 million in the mid-1950s to nearly $400 million in the early 1970s, the public share of that total grew from about one-eighth to one-third.

Increasing public control of new development also marked the period of suburban maturation. At the beginning of the postwar boom, fewer than half a dozen suburban communities had any semblance of zoning, subdivision regulations, capital improvement plans, or comprehensive planning commissions. By the early 1960s, of roughly fifty municipalities comprising the area inside the frontier of low density settlement, only three had not yet undertaken at least some of those programs. Meanwhile, to coordinate these local efforts, the state legislature had established the Metropolitan Planning Commission in 1957. The commission was succeeded in the late 1960s by the more powerful Metropolitan Council. Each was the first agency of its kind in the United States. A 1962 survey showed that the

Twin Cities—along with Milwaukee—led the large metropolitan areas of the Midwest in per capita commitment of money and manpower to comprehensive planning. All of those activities reflected the growth of governmental controls over land development and the efforts of both local governments and the larger metropolis to monitor physical change and program public investments. Those commitments grew out of the experiences of both voters generally and community leaders in particular during the chaotic years of explosive residential development.

But figures on governmental efforts tell only part of the story. During the period of maturation, large developers have accounted for an increasing share of total building. Because they have controlled large and diverse tracts of land and large amounts of front-end capital, they have been able to package more comprehensively planned communities. Those efforts have been further encouraged by high land costs and high construction costs. So the integrated design of residential, commercial, and open space over large areas has come from private as well as public initiative.

The end result has been that "planning" has become a symbolic term—perhaps also a buzz-word—in suburban development in the 1960s and 1970s—planned communities, planned unit developments, planned residential clusters, planned garden apartments, planned shopping centers, planned educational centers, planned industrial parks, planned mobile home communities, and so on.

The system of freeways and expressways was probably the single most important new ingredient introduced into the suburbs from the late 1950s to the early 1970s. In a general way, those roads greatly increased the overall speed and capacity of transportation. Their effect in the Twin Cities was perhaps even greater than it was in many other metropolitan areas of comparable size. The Twin Cities area built more miles of freeway per capita than any other metropolis in the million or more class because the double downtowns called for two sets of radials rather than one.

But, in addition to its general effects, the freeway system also exerted a crucial influence on the location of all other new investments during this period. The radials reinforced the traditionally easy movement from the central business districts and the Midway district to suburban areas and drastically increased the distance to which activities linked to those districts could penetrate the countryside. The new circumferential routes opened extensive areas of woods and lakeshore in the voids between older radial spokes of growth. The circumferential routes also reduced the travel time between many suburbs by providing more direct routes between them. That was a decentralizing force, and decentralization was further accentuated by the creation of new major nodes in the metropolitan circulation system at the intersections of radial and circumferential freeways.

The freeways interacted with the new standards of affluence and the inertia of established metropolitan and regional markets to guide the location of new jobs and new homes during the period of suburban maturation.

Location of Burgeoning Employment

In 1950 suburban employment numbered about 90,000—roughly 20 percent of the metropolitan total. By 1970 the number of suburban jobs had grown to more than 350,000 and comprised more than 40 percent of the metropolitan total. To be sure, at least one-quarter of these new jobs were in scattered locations.

But much of the suburban employment boom was aggregated in a few major commercial and industrial districts. Several of those locations simply reflected expansion or relocation from the central business districts or the Midway district, across narrow barriers of railroad yards or older development, to nearby freeway interchange areas. Most important in that class are West Highway 55 (Golden Valley, Plymouth), West Highway 12 (Golden Valley, Plymouth, Minnetonka), Roseville-Arden Hills, and Maplewood.

Several of the largest Twin Cities–based corporations led the expansion from the central cities into these new districts. General Mills, Honeywell, and Gamble-Red Owl Stores shifted to the west from Minneapolis. Control Data, Univac, and a complex of trucking firms and suppliers shifted north from the Midway district to Roseville and Arden Hills. And the 3M Corporation built its new headquarters and research center in Maplewood, east of St. Paul. These locational decisions further reinforced the freeway development pattern. Because of the size or monumental nature of the investments and the number of work trips in-

volved, it was essential that the development plans be coordinated with regional transportation plans.

The general pattern of suburban employment growth reflected the century-old pull toward the south and west. Since the frontier of commercial agriculture passed westward across central Minnesota in the 1870s, the locational advantage for distribution firms serving the Upper Midwest region has been on the Minneapolis side of the metropolitan area. Each central city posed a barrier to the other in shipping to the outlying region, and most of the market lies to the west. Regional distributors and services look west and northwest to the Red River valley and the spring wheat region, south and southwest to the northern part of the Corn Belt in southern Minnesota, northern Iowa, eastern South Dakota, and northeast Nebraska.

This directional attraction continued in the era of suburbanization of regional branch offices, warehouses, and related banks, hotels, and restaurants. And it was reinforced by the chance location of the metropolitan airport on the broad outwash plain west of historic Fort Snelling. The result is that the major suburban employment concentrations are largest in the southwest quadrant. From Edina to the airport and extreme southwest corner of St. Paul, subdistricts and strips have coalesced into a new third center of the Twin Cities, comparable to downtown St. Paul in retail sales and office floor space. The new developments in this district have included many shifts or expansions from the central part of Minneapolis, but they have also included many new firms. There are hotels, branch offices, branch plants, retailers, corporate headquarters, and financial institutions—some locally based, some imported—which had not been located in the Twin Cities before.

Altogether, the dozen major suburban concentrations contain about two-thirds of the employment located within the area of post–World War II development—nearly a quarter of a million jobs. They embrace all of the eight major regional shopping malls, with 7.5 million square feet of floor space. They include ten of the eleven major concentrations of suburban offices, with 98 percent of the floor space, or about one-third of the modern office space in the metropolitan area. They also include about three-fifths of the suburban industrial park land, with nearly nine-tenths of the total industrial park land value. In fact, 48 percent of the total suburban industrial park land value is concentrated in the western part of the Edina-airport district—testimony to the pull of the market toward the southwest.

Meanwhile, office and industrial employment that is an integral part of the metropolitan system has grown throughout a zone of metropolitan influence far beyond the suburban belt twenty-five to sixty miles from the downtowns. Home offices of major corporations are dispersed widely through this zone. Most of these are homegrown manufacturing or financial firms, based on accessibility to regional markets, local surplus labor on farms and in small towns, and access to regional resources of management and financing. They tend to be located in or near the principal historic rural trade centers; hence they are also in the main highway and rail corridors. All of them are no farther in time from the Twin Cities airport than Westchester or Fairfield counties are from Kennedy Airport in New York.

Branch plant concentration coincides with the major area of industrial job growth. The pattern is most influenced by accessibility to Twin Cities markets and parent plants, although it is stretched somewhat toward the southwest by the rich farm equipment and supply market of the Corn Belt and northwest by a relatively abundant supply of underemployed farm labor in the marginal dairy country.

With both corporate offices and branch plants in the countryside, and major concentrations of job locations in the suburbs, suburbia and exurbia are integral parts of an extensive, evolving, interacting metropolitan system. Decentralization of employment locations has accompanied suburban maturation and rural assimilation and that decentralization has tended to equalize geographical accessibility to jobs for people who live in all parts of the metropolis. The average home-work trip from most suburban neighborhoods has increased from four to seven miles but is clearly less than the distance from that neighborhood to the nearer of the two central business districts or the Midway.

Location of the New Mix of Homes

To Twin Cities residents, lake shores and wooded hillsides are highly desirable places to live. They combine amenity and prestige in whatever combination one wishes. This view holds within any socioeconomic stratum or from any socioeconomic perspective. The completion of the modern arterial and freeway network in the late 1950s and 1960s opened up vast areas of rolling, lake-studded glacial moraine land which had not been nearly as accessible in earlier years. If the rough terrain and abundance of surface water forced higher land preparation, utility, and construction costs, those barriers fell easily before the unprecedented affluence of the times. The improved highway net and the search for amenity reinforced each other and residential development helped to set the trend away from flatland and railway or streetcar orientation toward moraine land and freeway orientation, and toward larger lots and lower densities for multiple as well as single family dwellings.

There was a new element in the pattern of residential development during this period and it probably has intensified since 1970. On the one hand, there was a record rate of low density expansion, with less contiguity—more leapfrogging—than ever before. At the same time, however, there was also a record rate of medium and high density fill-in of previously low density areas than ever before. The fill-in also showed less contiguity of development than in previous periods. About 70 percent of the new medium density development was adjacent to the contiguous medium and high density metropolitan mass; about 30 percent was not. The record rate of low density expansion and leapfrogging has been noted widely and with alarm. The record rate of fill-in has received much less attention.

The two phenomena probably reflect alternative responses of the housing industry and market to extreme cost increases for capital, land, and construction. Alternative courses of action have been (1) increase density—hence develop close-in locations where central sewer is available—or (2) reduce land costs—hence go farther out than ever before.

The trend is seen by numerous public agencies and organizations as portending a serious problem. The new islands of medium density have received extensions of the sewer network. As a result, sewer trunks crossed intervening areas of remaining low density and those areas now have both land and sewer available. Meanwhile, unsewered developments sprawl in low density islands far beyond the existing or contemplated sewer network. It is feared that those areas will fill in, and their residents will need sewers whose cost will greatly exceed the fiscal capability of the local residents and needlessly strain the resources of the metropolitan sewer board. Hence policies are evolving to inhibit further advances or leaps of the low density frontier and force new development to fill in areas adjacent to the contiguous urban mass or between certain new, medium density islands. The evolving policies favor the medium density approach to the cost squeeze, and discourage the cheap land, low density approach.

Notwithstanding the widespread image of suburbia as a homogeneous or monotonous mass, a vivid and complex regionalism appears to have developed, especially in the period of suburban maturation. The moraine areas—even the outwash plains—have tremendous internal physical diversity. The metropolitan area contains nearly 1,000 "recreational lakes"—so classified by the state Department of Natural Resources. But there are also many more hundreds of small ponds. Because of the detail of small knobs and kettles, the larger lakes have intricate shorelines, with countless bays and islands and varied vistas. The metropolis lies astride the major continental vegetation boundaries between forest and prairie and between broadleaf and coniferous forests. Hence there are rich maple-basswood-white oak forests, birch-aspen groves, ridges and islands of pine, tamarack bogs, and fields in former prairie openings bordering oak woodlands. And there are accompanying differences in bird and animal life.

The distribution of these diverse landscapes has the randomness and kaleidescopic detail with which the glaciers acquired and dumped their burden in the Ice Age. Most Twin Citians are keenly aware of these variations and have preferences among them. Hence the market for residential land and housing has reflected them down to their most minute details. The result is a great diversity and randomness of the residential landscape, with every conceivable combination of socioeconomic and physical features. This phenomenon is unquestionably a great leveler, though it mostly remains to be described and interpreted. If few suburban municipalities are homogeneous physically, few can be homogeneous in family income and related cultural attributes.

The suburban pattern of income differences is accompanied by many other cultural differences (Figure 25). Those also mainly await adequate study and definition. Cultural differences in the suburbs are probably as rich as those among the distinctive old neighborhoods of the central cities. To be sure, there is the concentration of Jewish people which suburbanized from North Minneapolis, or spilled over from the Kenwood district of Minneapolis, to eastern Golden Valley and St. Louis Park. And there is the relatively rapid diffusion and integration of middle income black families into the suburbs.

But most suburban cultural differences will not be found if they are sought in terms of the traditional measures of race, nationality, language, or religion. Yet as one walks and talks in the suburbs, the evidence is abundant that there are vivid and vitally important differences in diet, nutrition, drink, the nature and sources of information, parent-child relationships, family stability, health care, clothing, recreational expenditures. There are geographies of gardening, bowling, golfing, snowmobiling, boat ownership. Insofar as these are related to income, they reflect the intricate pattern of residential land values. But they are also related to values that lead some households to sacrifice for a lakeshore location, others to shun it—or lead to countless other kinds of locational decisions.

Great Variety in the Urbanizing Countryside

Beyond the suburbs, in the urbanizing countryside, the changing residential landscape tells yet another story. The part of this zone twenty-five to sixty miles from the downtowns has the highest percentage growth rates of population in the metropolitan system. The baby boom, housing boom, and schoolroom boom are making their last stand there. The most important factor is the population of local young people with traditional values, to some extent able to shelter those values by staying in their home communities, yet tapping into city-suburban affluence by means of long distance commuting. These people are mostly high school graduates. Hence most of their work trips lead to technical, clerical, or unskilled jobs. Their places of work are not only in the central cities and suburbs but also in the small towns and even in the open country—filling stations, taverns, gravel pits, for example—throughout the metropolitan region. They are mostly in the middle and lower middle income range.

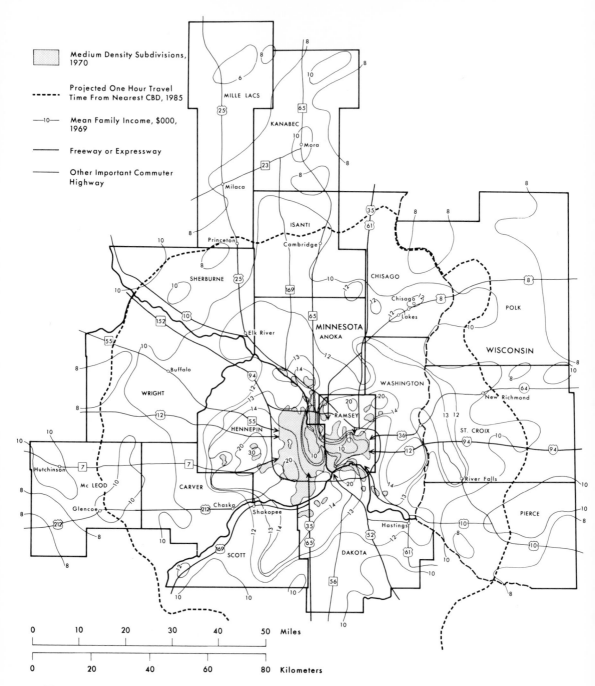

Figure 25. Family income variations in the Twin City area. Geographic variation of mean family income in the counties comprising the Twin City daily urban system.

Also contributing to growth in this zone are emigrants from the central cities and suburbs, making their deepest thrust into the countryside. The emigrants are a heterogeneous lot, with a very wide range of educational and occupational backgrounds, in the middle and upper middle income brackets. They are executives, proprietors, and professionals, to be sure; but the group also includes a wide variety of salespersons, tradesmen, office clerks, factory workers, and technicians. Some of the proprietors bring their small businesses with them into the countryside. For example one set up his metal fabricating plant in an abandoned creamery near his residential estate; another moved his cabinet shop from the city to a former dairy barn which he rents on a farm near his lake home. In turn, he has remodeled the lake home for comfortable year round occupance.

Finally, there is a growing accumulation of aging and elderly. These people are retired farmers and small town business operators, craftsmen, laborers, and housewives. They are mainly people who are not buying retirement in either an institution or a warmer climate. In most cases their savings are inadequate, though that factor is often reinforced by emotional attachment to the locale. The local retirees are augmented by immigrants who come not only from the Twin Cities but also from other parts of the Midwest, especially Iowa and the industrial cities of Illinois and Indiana. To serve this population there is an expansion of clinic and nursing home facilities comparable to the boom in school classrooms.

New householders in the urbanization zone are creating a rich variety of housing. There is a remodeling boom, with much of the work being done by the residents themselves. Old farmsteads are being remodeled as single family homes. Old houses in the small towns are being remodeled as single family homes or apartment buildings. So are abandoned one or two room schoolhouses in the countryside and old stores at rural crossroads or on the main streets of small hamlets. Mobile homes are situated in farmyards, on small town lots, in courts large and small—usually in the open country or at least beyond the edges of small towns—in subdivisions of one to five acre lots, on lakeshore land, in ten or twenty acre woodlots—perhaps gifts from retiring farmers to their newly married children. Precut houses ranging in size from two to five bedrooms are popular and it is common for the owner and his relatives to provide most of the labor for both the foundation and finishing. Owner-built homes are also common. Their designs are usually conventional, but distinctive features ranging from the ingenious to the outlandish are not uncommon. Finally, there are also conventionally built dwellings ranging from modest to elaborate.

Outbuildings are common. Many are for horses, which are luxury items—though kept by families in a very wide range of incomes. Many outbuildings are for trucks—incidental to the livelihood of so many laborers and tradesmen. But many outbuildings also house a true farming enterprise. For the region has a distinctive kind of suburbanization and intensification of its agriculture. Productivity of farmland ranks among the highest in Minnesota, although the soil quality is only mediocre. Yet the proportion of part time farmers is also among the highest in the state. It is a region of relatively intensive part time farming. It is not uncommon to see a farmer plowing or harvesting by tractor headlight after a day's work at the factory bench, grease rack, or supply room counter.

Population growth areas in the zone of urbanization appear not only on a map of population change but also on the map of family income. For growth is occurring mostly where long distance commuting or branch plants of metropolitan industries are contributing to the basic income. The location of those areas is partly correlated with highway access to city and suburban employment centers. But the pattern is greatly modified by the local patterns of lakeshore and wooded hills and also by accessibility to local employment centers.

There is some concern that exurban settlement will usurp the resource of open land that now surrounds the suburbs and central cities. There is some truth to this. In a way, there is an abundance of open space—about 5,000 square miles without significant development within an hour's driving time of the central business district or the Midway. That is enough to accommodate six to ten centuries of growth even at low outer suburban densities and recent metropolitan population increase rates. On the other hand, if that open space were divided into parcels averaging eight acres, it would last only about a decade at recent growth rates. The latter version of the process is probably nearer reality. Meanwhile, however, there are more than 100,000 acres of public open space within the one hour driving time zone. The newly created Metropolitan Parks and Open Space Board, under the Metropolitan Council, has been given $40 million dollars in bonding power by the Minnesota legislature, and much of the acquisition under that program will be in the exurban zone. Furthermore, key legislative and agency studies have shown that most of the overcrowded state park facilities are in the metropolitan zone of urbanization; hence future state acquisition and protection programs are likely to have a major focus in that area, as well.

Cultural differences also enrich the internal geography of the zone of urbanization. In one sense, the whole zone is a cultural region. For now, at least, it is a unique zone of interaction between city and country. Also, most residents still combine the culture of past rural isolation with the energy of newly increased affluence. Hence, many church congregations are swelling —buildings new structures or enlarging old ones. The zone contains Minnesota's largest concentration of old-time ballrooms, for it has the largest concentration of people who have both the taste for old-time music and the money for live entertainment. The Minnesota Orchestra can attract 2,000 local people to an outdoor symphony in a small town while, not far away, a steam threshing bee in an abandoned farmyard draws 3,000 from the countryside and the suburbs.

Cultural subregions, based on national background and religion, are as vivid in this zone as they are in the older neighborhoods of the central cities, although some are rapidly fading as they are diluted by immigration from the cities and suburbs. Two noteworthy examples are German Catholic concentrations—one centered on the Crow River valley communities of Hanover, Albertville, and St. Michael, along the boundary between Hennepin and Wright Counties; the other around Miesville and New Trier west of Hastings in Dakota County. Among all of the rural areas at similar distance from the central cities, those two were the last to shift their predominant economy out of farming and join the army of rural commuters. Other examples are the Bohemian community, which extends southward from Prior Lake in southern Scott County to New Prague; the French-Canadian community focused on Centerville and Hugo, north of White Bear Lake; and the historic Swedish community centered on the Chisago Lakes area and northern Washington County—scene of the American portions of Moberg's famous novels, *The Immigrants* and *Unto a New Land.*

Racially the urbanization zone is virtually all white. At the time of the 1970 census nonwhites numbered only about 3,000 out of roughly 800,000 total population in the zone. Perhaps it is noteworthy that more than 80 percent of the nonwhite population growth in the preceding decade occurred in towns with either a branch plant of a major national corporation or a college—both institutions highly sensitive to national and organized social pressures.

JUDGMENT DAY APPROACHES

Reviewing the landscapes that have emerged in the Twin Cities suburbs and beyond since 1945, one can recite the full litany of sins of American suburbia and exurbia. The region is fragmented into scores of autonomous local governments. Its ragged frontier of urbanization, low density, and commuters living sixty miles out are proof of urban sprawl. Many, if not all, of the suburban communities have grown with an imbalance between residential and nonresidential development. Some are almost entirely residential; others heavily commercial or industrial. Hence there are unbalanced community tax bases— some have the advantage of large nonresidential valuations to help the residents pay for municipal services; in others the residents have had to go it alone. The streetcar system was dismantled and the bus system was neglected until very recently. There was neglect of public open space acquisition for many years. There is little public low and moderate income housing outside the central cities. Racial segregation has produced minority ghettoes and virtually all-white neighborhoods.

We now appear to be leaving the era that spawned suburbia and exurbia and entering a new one. The population explosion and the affluent society are, respectively, awash in heavy seas of unprecedented contraception and inflation. The nation is evolving a new perspective on energy consumption in particular and resource consumption in general. That, too, seems certain to affect housing costs, style, and location.

As Twin Citians approach the day of atonement for this age in the life of their metropolis, how will their sins be judged by that Great Urban Model in the Sky?

Priorities and Increasing Management
The post–World War II growth ring of the Twin Cities was built in less than three decades to accommodate a million people. At the minimum, that has been a very large and rapid accomplishment. By comparison, the Minnesota Experimental City—acclaimed as a bold pro-

posal—was to reach a population of one-quarter million in one decade.

Nor was the expansion totally undisciplined. At the beginning of the epoch a large and fast-growing population, with a particular legacy of circumstances from the war-Depression years, was faced with an immediate task and finite resources. In retrospect it is apparent that there were priorities and a crude order of procedure. The community addressed the necessary tasks in the following chronological order: (1) housing and elementary schools; (2) streets, sewers, and highways; (3) commercial and industrial buildings; (4) hospitals, high schools, and churches; and, finally, (5) junior colleges and vocational schools, government and business offices, public open space acquisition and improvement. There were also priorities within each of those broad tasks. For example, single family homes dominated production overwhelmingly during the years when demand was concentrated in young households with a very high birth rate. Then apartment construction escalated when demand shifted heavily toward retirement households and young households with a very low birth rate.

Although the tasks were initiated in chronological order, the effort on each of them has continued once it was begun. Nevertheless, peak years of activity on each task tended to follow soon after its initiation.

Suppose a suitable comprehensive model of urban development and operation had existed in 1945. Suppose further that all of the necessary data had been available and had been collected and entered. And suppose that the consequences of alternative strategies of investment and regulation had been considered and voted upon. In retrospect, again, it is quite plausible that the general priorities and procedures might not have been greatly different from those which actually occurred. One wonders if more "balance" between one family and multiple dwellings would have been acceptable to the people who needed new housing in the late 1940s and 1950s. If the model indicated that more "balance" between housing construction, municipal capital improvements, and nonresidential building would have slowed rectification of the housing shortage and raised prices, would the majority of households have voted for more "balance"? Would abstinence from the automobile, and accompanying pre-Depression residential densities, have been ac-ceptable to a middle income majority in need of housing—given the available data and theory on energy pricing and supplies in 1946 (or twenty years later)?

In short, individual priorities were clear and not hard to justify. They were aggregated into collective priorities through the discipline imposed by the market for labor, materials, land, and money—all in a crude but recognizable way.

Meanwhile, the community has gradually increased the *management* of this expansion process as experience has accumulated. The examples are abundant—metropolitanwide coordination of zoning, hospital planning, solid waste management; metropolitan financing and operation of airports, sewers, and transit; metropolitanwide financing of regional parks; metropolitanwide organizations of county officials, open housing advocacy groups, school officials, and many others. Zoning is becoming increasingly influenced by the timing and location of public capital improvement programs. Performance requirements are increasingly used in connection with zoning to bring aesthetics into the landscape.

The reasons for this increasing management are fundamental. The metropolitan area and its component communities have monitored the changing postwar settlement. They have done it rather poorly, but with gradually growing sophistication. The job has been done by a loose consortium of public agencies, private utilities, scholars and teachers, and citizens organizations. As those groups have monitored and publicized their findings, the general understanding of both the evolving metropolis and its evolving problems has also grown.

The Twin Cities and Minnesota have attracted national attention for their approaches to problems of metropolitan development. It may well be true that the significant accomplishment thus far has not been so much in the anticipation of future problems and preparing for them in advance as it has been in rather quickly grasping current problems and responding to them as an intelligent community.

Nagging Questions

Some questions have been especially stubborn. They were on the public agenda at the beginning of the postwar epoch, they are not yet resolved, and they are likely to persist into the next epoch.

1. On many sides, advocates of local government reorganization argue that the crazy-quilt pattern and multiplicity of local governments in the metropolitan region is irrational and costly. In what ways is that true? Does each different service provided by local government have its own unique optimal service area (threshold and range), unrelated to the vagaries of muncipal and county boundaries? If that is the case, can those services ever be rationalized without establishing special or consolidated districts, separate from the general units of local government—the counties and municipalities? And what then is the appropriate function of the counties and municipalities?

2. Proponents of growth control argue that sprawl is bad because extra costs to the people who do it are borne not by the sprawlers but by the people who live in closer in, higher density areas. Commonly used illustrations are the costs of road improvements and maintenance, school busing, or sewer lines. The questions are: Who is actually subsidized now? By whom? Where? How much? Until those questions are answered it is only frustrating to try to establish equity on the basis of theory. Once the actual situation is well described, it will be much simpler for public officials and their constituents to respond to the ultimate question: Which parts of the system should be subsidized? Where? By whom? Why?

3. It has been observed earlier that evolving policies tend to favor the high density approach to the housing cost squeeze and to discourage the cheap land approach. Yet, important cost-cutting innovations—actual or potential—have been permitted on the low density frontier or beyond, while they have tended to be discouraged or prohibited in the more developed and institutionalized suburbs and central cities. Notable cases are factory-assembled, precut, and owner-built houses. As more sophisticated innovations come in construction, sanitation, or space heating, there will be more need than ever for people and places willing and able to do the testing. What zone will perform the essential experimental and safety valve functions of the relatively unregulated frontier under conditions of controlled growth?

4. Multiple agencies of government have evolved out of the experience of three decades of fast growth. They have responsibility for regulation in the fields of natural resources or environment, health, education, human relations, welfare, and transportation. Their powers are defined and isolated by thousands of pieces of legislation. Yet, their responsibilities within the metropolitan region are interrelated in thousands of ways. For almost any problem that arises, there are existing agencies and powers that can move toward its solution, but such action is almost certain to require coordinated use of multiple powers by multiple agencies. That situation will occur no matter how the agencies are realigned or redefined, for each problem tends to be both complex and unique. The question is: How are these many agencies and laws to be effectively coordinated?

5. Finally, if a new epoch is indeed now breaking upon us, what are going to be the distinctive and important characteristics of that epoch? What will be the resultant major problems of metropolitan operation and the inherent solutions? Which of today's problems in the post–World War II growth rings will—whether they are solved or not—be quietly replaced by new problems of greater urgency in the new epoch?

How, then, will the Twin Citians' postwar development effort be judged? Perhaps it will be on how they met the need to monitor, change, carry on informed discussion, develop understanding, and discipline their response to the problems and issues they perceived. Perhaps Twin Citians in the new epoch will be judged according to their effort to further improve those activities and their ability to respond to tomorrow's problems more quickly and effectively than they did to yesterday's.

Bibliography

Blegen, Theodore C. *Minnesota: A History of the State.* Minneapolis: University of Minnesota Press, 1963.

Borchert, John R. *The Twin Cities.* New York: Doubleday and Company, 1959.

——. "The Twin Cities Urbanized Area: Past, Present, Future." *Geographical Review* 51 (1961): 47–70.

Borchert, J.R., and R.B. Adams. *Trade Centers and Trade Areas of the Upper Midwest.* Urban Report no. 3. Minneapolis: Upper Midwest Economic Study, 1963.

Borchert. John R., and Donald P. Yaeger. *Atlas of Minnesota Resources and Settlement.* Minneapolis: University of Minnesota Department of Geography, 1968.

Brown, Ralph H. *Historical Geography of the United States.* New York: Harcourt, Brace and Company, 1948.

Gras, N.S.B. "The Significance of the Twin Cities for Minnesota History." *Minnesota History* 7 (1926): 3–17.

Hart, John Fraser, and Russell B. Adams. "Twin Cities." *Focus* 20, 6 (February 1970): 1–11.

Hartshorne, Richard. "The Twin City District: A Unique Form of Urban Landscape." *Geographical Review* 22 (1932): 431–42.

Henderson, J.M.; A.O. Krueger; R.S. Rodd; and J.S. Adams. *National Growth and Economic Change in the Upper Midwest.* Minneapolis: University of Minnesota Press, 1965.

Lukermann, Fred E. "The Changing Pattern of Flour Mill Location." *The Northwestern Miller,* Vol. 261, nos. 3, 4, 6, 8, 12, 13, 17 (1959).

Robinson, Edward Van Dyke. *Early Economic Conditions and the Development of Agriculture in Minnesota.* University of Minnesota, Studies in the Social Sciences no. 3. Minneapolis: University of Minnesota Press, 1915.

Schmid, Calvin F. *Social Saga of Two Cities.* Minneapolis, 1937.

Schwartz, George M., and George A. Thiel. *Minnesota's Rocks and Waters.* Minneapolis: University of Minnesota Press, 1963.

WPA Writers Project. *Minneapolis: The Story of a City.* Minneapolis, 1940.

About the Authors

John S. Adams, A Minneapolis native, graduated in economics from the College of St. Thomas, received a masters degree in economics from the University of Minnesota, and completed the doctorate in geography at the University of Minnesota. His interest in urban and regional analysis developed while he was a member of the research staff of the Upper Midwest Economic Study. After teaching four years at the Pennsylvania State University, he returned to the University of Minnesota in 1970 where he is now professor of geography and public affairs. His writings focus on urban residential structure, urban housing markets, intra-urban migration, and comparative analysis of American urban areas. Since 1970 he has been research director of the Association of American Geographers' Comparative Metropolitan Analysis Project.

John R. Borchert was graduated from DePauw University in geology, and earned masters and doctoral degrees in geography at the University of Wisconsin at Madison. He was urban research director of the Upper Midwest Economic Study, and has authored many articles and monographs in the fields of urbanization and the spatial dimensions of public policy issues in resource utilization. He has served as consultant or as board member of many local, state, and federal agencies. A longtime resident of the Twin Cities, he is currently professor of geography and Director of the Center for Urban and REgional Affairs at the University of Minnesota.

Ronald Abler received his B.A., M.A. and Ph.D. in geography from the University of Minnesota. He has been a Visiting Professor at the University of British Columbia and at the University of Minnesota.

Professor Abler's primary research and teaching interests are in Urban Geography and in the Geography of Communications Systems, and in the relationship between the two. Aside from his work on the Comparative Metropolitan Analysis Project, he has most recently been concerned with tradeoffs between transportation and communication, the possibilities of substituting communication for transportation, and the effects of such tradeoffs and substitutions on settlement forms.